SELF-HYPN
FOR LIF_

The Author

Dr Tracie O'Keefe DCH, BA, N-SHAP Adv Dip Thp MCRAH is a clinical hypnotherapist, psychotherapist and counsellor at the London Medical Centre in Harley Street. She gained her degree and doctorate in clinical hypnotherapy with the American Institute of Hypnotherapy and took post-graduate advanced diplomas in hypnosis and psychotherapy at the National School of Hypnosis and Advanced Psychotherapy in London. As well as running a busy practice, she spends a great deal of time researching, writing and lecturing about human behaviour and campaigning for human rights. Her professional memberships include Central Register of Advanced Hypnotherapists and British Register of Complementary Practitioners.

Katrina Fox (Editor) is a journalist and editor. Among the areas she covers are social welfare and social justice issues, human and animal rights, sexuality, gender issues, veganism and complementary health. She is the co-author of the book *Trans-X-U-All: The Naked Difference* and is actively involved in campaigning to end all forms of animal abuse.

This book is dedicated to members of all movements for world peace and compassion to all sentient beings everywhere, and posthumously to Timothy Leary, who stood for a person's freedom to explore their own mind, unfettered by the establishment

Self-Hypnosis for Life
Mind, Body & Spiritual Excellence

Dr Tracie O'Keefe DCH
Edited by Katrina Fox

Published by:
Extraordinary People Press
1B Portman Mansions
Chiltern Street
London W1M 1PX
Tel. 020 7935 4490
Fax. 020 7486 5998
E-mail katfox@easynet.co.uk
Website http://easyweb.easynet.co.uk/~katfox/extra1.htm

First published 2000

British Library Cataloguing-in-Publication Data
A catalogue record for this book is available from the British Library

ISBN 0 9529482 3 0

Cover designed by William Rood

Printed by Palladian Press, Great Britain

Distributed in the UK by Turnaround

Go inside and imagine how it would be if you were exquisite at self-hypnosis

By the same author:

Trans-X-U-All: The Naked Difference
ISBN 09529482 0 6

Investigating Stage Hypnosis
ISBN 09529482 1 4

Sex, Gender & Sexuality: 21st Century Transformations
ISBN 09529482 2 2

Published by Extraordinary People Press

CONTENTS

Acknowledgements

In writing this book I would like to give thanks to all those who taught me hypnosis by their actions or writings. The four hypnotherapists I would like to give special thanks to are **Ray Keedy-Lilley**, **Pamela Gawler-Wright**, **Caroline Miller** and **Michael Joseph**, who each in their own way, have taught me a great deal unconsciously.

I would also like to pay homage to the writings of **Milton Erickson**, **Ernest Rossi**, **D Corydon Hammond**, **Richard Bandler**, **John Grinder**, **Vernon Coleman, Timothy Leary** and many others who have, through their works, cast light on my way.

A special thank you goes to all my clients and others who have allowed themselves to be mentioned within these pages, whose identities have been changed to protect their right to privacy.

Finally I would also like to thank my research assistant **Gerald Franklin** and my beloved partner and editor **Katrina Fox**, whose hard work and suggestions have been invaluable.

Preface

As a beautiful spring day rises over a blue English skyline I sit down to start this work, wanting to pass onto you my enthusiasm about self-hypnosis and the very joy of being alive. It is not that I am the ever optimistic fool, although sometimes I might be, but that I have learnt many skills about hypnosis, living, surviving and prospering that I use with and teach to my clients. These self-hypnosis techniques help people resolve outstanding issues and move forward to have a sense of personal well-being.

You could be forgiven for thinking that I am a little ray of sunshine who insensitively chirps on. You could even be forgiven for thinking that because I am a therapist you would expect me to be all resources and smiles. The reality is that earlier in my life I knew despair, anger, loneliness and feelings of being abandoned. But not for a long time now – not since I learned how to rely on myself through self-hypnosis to supply almost everything I need – that is everything my mind needs to create my inner well being and find a centred place to live.

In today's fast-moving world, modern life makes ever increasing demands on all of us, with people becoming stressed, depressed, and disconnected from their families. Due to the pressure of just making a living some people get left with little time to spend with friends or forget about having fun. The World Health Organisation predicts that in the early part of the 21st century depression will be one of the most common causes of illness, just below coronary heart disease or AIDS.

Hypnosis has been used for thousands of years to help people in every walk of life to gain mastery over illnesses, elevate their minds, emotions and intellect. Today hypnosis is undergoing a massive growth as medicine, psychology, healing and education realise its incredible potential to help people fulfil their maximum abilities and dreams.

This is a book that helps the novice to understand self-hypnosis to help themselves and in turn help others too. As you learn more about how to apply self-hypnosis to your life you will feel the power of being in control of your thoughts, emotions and experiences. Not only will it give you a greater freedom to choose the way you live but it will also teach you to constantly achieve states of physical, mental and spiritual excellence.

Dr Tracie O'Keefe DCH, May 2000

How to Use This Book

Since this work is so full of many different self-hypnosis techniques I want you to treat it like a sumptuous buffet of life enhancing and changing experiences. You can start from the beginning and take your time working your way progressively through each section, trying every exercise, and you can also go back to anything you did before to help improve what you are or will be doing later.

Out of confusion will grow new learnings and remember, confusion always comes before learning. Take your time to enjoy the whole experience as you immerse yourself in the routine of using self-hypnosis daily and trust your unconscious to help you. Let this work become your companion, giving it a favourite place to live where you can come into contact with it and dip into it whenever you need, want or desire.

Some techniques will work immediately for you and others will require you to practise them again and again. As you break through new barriers to go onto higher levels of your own personal development the rewards will pay off handsomely in different areas of your life for many years ahead.

You may find yourself facing truths that you have been trying to ignore for years and having to deal with unfinished business that you have never before had the courage to sort out. Some people are initially unsure whether such a high level of good living is really happening to them or whether they are deluding themselves. If that happens, push on relentlessly until you become used to the idea that you are definitely more than you ever consciously envisaged you could be.

Nothing in this work will cause you pain or sorrow as I just never saw the need for that kind of therapy. Yes...sometimes feeling different will be weird but so was learning to ride a bicycle, taking your first steps or beginning to speak, until you got used to them.

When you go on to make personal tapes for trance inductions with the scripts, please keep them strictly to yourself and out of the reach of other people. They will only be relevant to your life and should never be used by anyone else, so if you have finished with them, wipe them clean or throw them away. Do not play such tapes when you are in the car or operating any kind of machinery but only when you are in private and can completely relax. Do not go into a hypnotic trance when you are working and have responsibilities to which you need to attend.

At the end of each chapter is a list of books for further reading which can be ordered from your local bookshop or library. If they are unavailable or out of print you can find similar books to help you along your journey of self-discovery and development, and remember: knowledge is power.

In the exercises section are many mind-expanding and thought-provoking questionnaires for you to fill in. These are an important part of the book because they teach you to look at your motivations, behaviours, attitudes and possible potentials. Treat this section as a way of looking consciously at what you are learning unconsciously about yourself as you become more proficient at self-hypnosis.

This is a compendium that teaches you self-hypnosis and its uses, which cannot be skim-read as you need to deeply involve yourself in the process as taught within these pages. Read the text many times and go back to it whenever you want to brush up on your self-hypnosis techniques. If you need extra help take the book to a well respected and qualified clinical hypnotherapist and ask them for tuition. And most of all, above everything else, remember...The Number One Rule of Life...

HAVE FUN!

One night, just after the beginning of the world, the Sunbird was sitting on the moon because the sun had gone away again. The Sunbird did not need to sleep, just like the sun, and it was so polite it did not want to offend the moon as it knew it was the only company the moon had.

The Sunbird, in boredom during the night, often drew faces on the moon for the want of something better to do. Most of all it loved to spread its magic wings during daylight and fly in the sky, casting all the known colours across the earth as the sun shone throughout its rainbow coloured wings. Red for poppies, blue for the oceans, and yellow for dancing daffodils that mixed together in millions of different hues.

That night the Sunbird for the first time fell asleep and dreamt the crescent shape of the moon had become too small and it had fallen off, flying into the horizon to chase the sun. The Sunbird flew and flew and flew until it caught the sun up and cast the light of the rainbow through its wings to the earth. Suddenly they flew together, as they had never done before, one in unison with the other, around and around the earth forever, smiling at the moon as it passed them each night.

Chapter One

Learning Self-Hypnosis, Finding Your Centre & The Way of Peace

What I have learnt and will teach you is that life's abilities and happiness start...FROM THE INSIDE OUTWARDS...and you may be thinking that is a funny thing to say, but as you learn more about self-hypnosis it will become clearer. In a world that is obsessed with consumerism – having the fastest car, biggest house, flashiest diamonds, fattest wallet – anything beyond basic pleasant comfort, safety, relationships and intellectual stimulation is largely superfluous.

Your greatest possession is, without a shadow of a doubt, your...**IMAGINATION**...which costs you nothing to use yet can give you more than anything that you can buy in any store. While your imagination is your greatest resource it is often the most underused in modern society because we have become accustomed to being passively entertained through the likes of television, films and radio.

Just recently my mother gave me my school report from 40 years ago which said: "This child has too much imagination." What a silly thing to say about someone who was going to be a hypnotherapist...don't you think? And I laughed, and laughed some more, thinking that the teacher who wrote such a careless and destructive comment might not have known how to laugh as much as me.

The Buddhists say that out of humility can grow greatness and in many ways I agree with them. In order to learn something you must know nothing to begin with, and to know nothing is an advantage when wanting to learn a great deal, which could eventually lead to wisdom (the kingdom of knowing). So we all come from humility and should we ever forget that, we are foolish because we have forgotten the advantages and pleasures of having a great deal to learn.

In today's world we are pushed and pulled by people wanting to sell us a piece of anything and everything. The tribesperson in the desert wants a colour television, even when they may not have electricity, because they are afraid of missing out. People want more money because they are afraid of being ill and left to suffer a horrible death in poverty, pain, loneliness and old age. Yet in a society that truly cared for its poor, disadvantaged, old and infirm, this would never happen.

Some people often become overwhelmed by life and feel that the ever increasing pace is dragging them along as they break down and suffer collapses in their mind, emotions and personal relationships. It all becomes too much and they withdraw, become ill, consumed with feelings of hopelessness about themselves and the lack of possibilities in their future. To say they become mentally ill is far too judgemental for me because I like to think of life as a series of...**ACTIVE STAGES**...and...**RESTING STAGES**. Sometimes people just need to withdraw from the rat race, recover, rest or have fun before going on to their next active stage.

For people who may be susceptible to cancer and auto-immune diseases like myalgic encephalomyelitis (ME), not listening to your internal signals telling you...**IT'S TIME TO TAKE TIME OUT**...eventually causes illness. If you listen very carefully to your body, it talks to you as it gives you a level of stress that is a signal for you to change your strategies. Unnecessary and excess stress occurs when a person does not make those changes, but ignores the signals and continues along a course that is no longer appropriate for them.

Unnatural levels of stress caused by war, too much work and studying, poor relationships or living arrangements cause the body to work overtime. In such cases the body eventually pulls the plug on the person's activation systems. The whole body then enforces rest by preventing the person from operating well for weeks, months or even years at a time.

So many people who succumbed to cancer can trace back the kind of lifestyle or trauma that typically led to their body's defences operating at a lower level. Nature knows how to heal but the kind of lives we are often leading in the modern western world do not allow that healing to happen effectively.

Most of the people who come into my clinic have failed to move on when an old strategy comes to the end of its natural life. They have not developed or implemented new and different strategies to take them forward in ways that are right and conducive to them in the present or future. Although I am a highly skilled doctor in my field, my job in essence is quite simple because what I do is help people to move forward when they are stuck to reach their next level of self-evolution.

It gives me such an enormous amount of pleasure seeing people beginning to rectify their own lives after only a few sessions. I love to watch them become empowered through hypnosis and learning life skills to live their lives fully, and most of all remembering the number one rule of life...**HAVE FUN!**

Short-termism was the greatest theme of the 20th century. Everyone wanted it today just in case stocks ran out and there would be none left. The slash and burn sale at the end of the second millennium was quick, get a piece of everything in your living room today and take as much debt as you would like to pay for it.

More than half the planet inherited third world debts that were designed to stop them from prospering and competing economically with the very people who lent them money in the first place. Some wealthy countries wiped out debts for some poor countries in 2000 but not nearly enough to make a real difference to world poverty.

The mortgage and credit card was invented for the commoner, which replaced tied cottages and it invented slavery of another kind, ensuring that the proletariat would know his or her place and keep it. One of the modern day formulas is often work, sleep, earn, pay debts and repeat. And even though the rich part of the world focuses on consumerism, more than three quarters of people on the planet have never even used a telephone.

What happened to lazy days, dangling your toes in the stream of life on hot summer afternoons? Wandering like a vagabond from rootless dale, glen and clifftop to some hazy distant place? It has become a crime in many places to be without a number bearing your identity, bar code, microchip or name tag. In our attempt to create freedom humankind ironically has created new kinds of prisons.

So…**GO INSIDE AND IMAGINE**…because it is ever easier to do with practice. Imagine you can actually have control over your own life, body, emotions, values, attitudes, beliefs and fate. Reclaim your ownership of yourself. The most profound and marvellous thing I have learnt as a hypnotist and therapist is that people are amazing. Every week I am privileged enough to watch clients sit in my office and change to such an extent they turn their lives around in ways they had only ever previously dreamed possible.

People can gain strength to squarely face their demons, confront them, overcome them and discover that they can be the champions of their own lives. It is a wonderful thing to become your own hero or heroine as a first step…**HYPNOSIS IS ONE OF THE STRONGEST WAYS TO CHANGE YOUR MIND**…**THOUGHTS**…**EMOTIONS**…**AND BEHAVIOURS**.

Your belief in the rightness of the outcomes achieved by your actions can be strong, centred, calm, focused, relaxed, leaving you smiling, and even laughing. Turn each event in your life into an opportunity. What might have been a disaster can actually be turned into a huge asset by teaching yourself how to be even more strong in your belief in yourself…**TURN WHATEVER HAPPENS TO YOU INTO A LEARNING EXPERIENCE THAT CAN POSITIVELY TEACH YOU SOMETHING**.

For many thousands of years in China, Ancient Egypt, Greece, Persia, and all the way through history, hypnosis has been used to help people come into contact with their inner resources. In the 18th century in France, Anton Mesmer made hypnosis popular again under the name of animal magnetism. Today, hypnotherapists, doctors, psychologists, psychiatrists, psychotherapists, counsellors, and different kinds of therapists help their clients by teaching them self-hypnosis.

USE SELF-HYPNOSIS TO CREATE AND RECREATE YOURSELF

Here when I talk about self-hypnosis I take in what some people refer to as a trance-like state, meditation, visualisation, reverie or a state of being other than consciousness. This does not include deep sleep because that is not a trance state, although very deep hypnosis may resemble deep sleep. Many clients often say they are worried about whether they are doing the self-hypnosis right, to which I tell them...**YOUR UNCONSCIOUS KNOWS WHAT TO DO SO LET IT GUIDE YOU**.

People naturally go into trances all the time as they drift off out of conscious attention and seem absent from the outside world. There may be times when you have done things automatically, without being consciously aware what you were doing, and you were in a trance. You are in a kind of trance when you are watching television, listening to the radio, driving a car, reading or any action where you are focusing your attention. The difference with self-hypnosis is that you are bringing on a trance by focusing the attention inside yourself.

Trance is the state you achieve and hypnosis is the action you take to create the trance state. When hypnotists take people into trances it is called hetero-hypnosis and when people take themselves into trances it is called auto-hypnosis or self-hypnosis.

What Einstein, the great inventor Anton Tesler, the world's foremost hypnotist of the 20th century Dr Milton Erickson and many other premier thinkers have understood is that reality has its limitations. The human mind, however, is a rich source of creation and if you can imagine anything inside your head when you are in a trance you are halfway there to making it happen.

Your unconscious mind works on imagining impulses that drive your body and life forward. If you can learn to harness your imagination, your intelligence and abilities will shoot off the scale. People are only limited by the prisons they create in their own minds, so for a moment think about some of the prisons you have created for yourself in your life.

REMEMBER...IMAGINATION IS THE KEY...

What is the Conscious and Unconscious?
The conscious and unconscious are metaphors for the way we view the function, quantity and qualities of the mind. They are philosophical estimates for the thought patterns that are going on in our minds throughout the whole of our life.

You can think of the conscious mind being like the hallway in a house and the unconscious being like the rest of the house. You have to go through the conscious mind to get to the house (unconscious) but you cannot store or use everything there. It is very useful for keeping things out of the house that you do not want and letting in things you do. The conscious mind is very small in comparison with the unconscious and only has a memory of about 20 to 30 seconds. It is like the immediate program you are running on the screen of a computer, our link with, and filter system protecting us against the outside world.

The unconscious mind is much greater in size, therefore more intelligent and can be likened to the whole of the rest of the house. It runs our bodies and remembers every single thing that has happened to us, storing all that information away until we need it. We may not be consciously aware that we have all those memories but we do. Because the unconscious is much smarter it often protects the conscious mind by keeping from it the things that it does not need to know or deal with.

Both the conscious and unconscious minds work in tandem to create and activate the whole personality. What we do when we induce trances with hypnosis is directly access the unconscious mind and all its resources, bypassing the conscious mind.

Six Pointers for Self-Hypnosis

1. As you work your way through this book you come to what are called scripts. You can follow the instructions and recite their contents to yourself inside your own head as you are going into and when you are in a trance.

2. Three dots (...) in the scripts mean that it is time to rest for three very long seconds to allow the last instruction or statement to be processed by your mind. Take your time, without hurrying, and allow a natural flow and meter to come to the way you make suggestions to yourself.

3. BOLD print letters in the script mean you will need to **EMPHASISE** that particular statement with an accent of importance above the rest of the script. The unconscious mind processes information in segments and likes to organise chunks of information before it goes onto the next important consideration. It gives emphasised communications priority.

4. Every script in this book is purposefully in the first person singular tense so you may quote it to yourself as written. It is designed for your unconscious to process the information as you are talking to yourself and to act directly on the instructions, ideas, and suggestions as given. When listening to a tape you have recorded...**REPEAT THE PHRASES TO YOURSELF**...inside your head after you have heard them spoken.

5. A post-hypnotic suggestion is when a suggestion is made to cause a behaviour to happen in the future, either at an appointed time or generally. It suggests an action that can, might or will happen in the near or far future.

6. An intra-hypnotic suggestion is when a suggestion is made to make a behaviour happen immediately within the trance experience. It will use verbs that pertain to present tense rather than future.

Do not worry whether you are doing it perfectly; practise each script several times, taking your time to enjoy the experience. Whenever you want to, you can go back to a script and go through it again, experiencing the positive benefits the scripts can induce in you. Practice requires you to make the trance experience a part of your daily schedule.

You can find a high-backed chair where your body weight is fully supported and your head and neck can rest comfortably...**YOUR LIMBS ARE UNCROSSED WITH YOUR PALMS FACING DOWN ON YOUR THIGHS**...this is where you can go into a trance. It is important to make yourself comfortable when doing self-hypnosis because you may be there for some time. Another alternative is to relax lying down with all your limbs uncrossed, with no twists in your back, but sitting up is preferable because you may fall asleep lying down.

Set the scene by taking the phone off the hook, putting the answer machine on and leaving the volume down. Write a notice for the room door you are using, asking that you not be disturbed and tell people you will not be available for this period. Close the door and make sure children and animals are in another part of the home.

Now I want you to find a tape recorder and record the various scripts in the book as you progress through it so that you can play them to yourself as you go into a trance. The other alternative is that you can learn the scripts by heart, reciting their contents to yourself, in your own voice inside your head, as you go into a trance.

If you are under a caring professional for any mental health problems or taking medication you should seek the advice of that professional before continuing. It may be that you can work with them as this book is designed for the general public, professional healthcarers, and for both to work together side by side. If you are left in any doubt, seek the help of a professional, well qualified and accredited clinical hypnotherapist. Do not assume because someone is a doctor, psychiatrist, psychologist, psychotherapist or counsellor that they are qualified in hypnosis as that may not be the case. Only work with hypnosis with people qualified in hypnosis.

REMEMBER...to tell yourself each time you go into a trance that you can wake up from the trance should there be any emergency, returning yourself fully to consciousness. Do that before you go into any self-hypnosis session and then forget about it consciously because your unconscious will remember for you.

REMEMBER...practice helps you become more confident in what you are doing and it is all right for you to join a self-hypnosis group, class, or even take a course given by well trained and professionally recognised hypnotherapist. Do not, however, have anything to do with stage hypnotists as they are rarely qualified as health professionals and the vast majority of hypnosis organisations do not allow them to be members. Professional healthcarers deplore the kind of dangerous, ridiculous antics those performers get up to and are constantly trying to get them banned.

I remember when my first great teacher of hypnosis asked me to go into my very first self-induced trance. I was not sure what I was doing but somehow over the next few days and weeks as I practised...**FOR 30 MINUTES EACH DAY**...it became routinely easier and the benefits started flooding into my life.

Dramatic Interpretation

When you are reading a script, reciting it inside your head, thinking of it or using your imagination, let those interpretations be dramatic. Life, after all, is a series of dramas which would be very boring if they all seemed the same. Also, be emotionally involved with your own acting-out, as we are each driven and led by our emotions which are very powerful and motivating.

The more dramatic and emotionally involved your interpretations are in trance, the more your unconscious will understand what you are communicating and find it motivating at an emotional as well as a thinking and behavioural level. By being dramatic I do not mean loud, but theatrical, and that sometimes means being quiet too. Bring out the thespian in you and seek to entertain your unconscious as well as influence its contents and processes.

The One to Eight Relaxation Method

This method of going into a self-hypnotic trance is one of the easiest and most relaxing ways for a person to learn self-hypnosis. The three following scripts consist of first going into a self-hypnotic, trance-like state; second finding your centre; and third a script that will guide you out of the hypnotic trance state back to wakefulness. It can be useful to count yourself out of trance by the reverse way you went in. If you are feeling at all tense before you go into a trance, clench all your muscles several times and then shake the tension out of them as you relax like a floppy rag doll.

As I said earlier you can record the scripts to begin with, leaving a two-minute gap between each script. Let the tape record two minutes of silence between each script so the sound of the on/off button does not jolt you out of trance. So you end up with one whole trance tape containing the three scripts. After a week of using the tape I want you to memorise the whole tape script and do away with the tape because the script needs to be part of your active thought processes.

Time your trances for about 25 to 30 minutes to begin with and as mentioned above, leave gaps of silence between each script as you rest in trance. When you are going into a trance without a tape it can be useful to set an alarm clock so you know the time to wake up out of trance. When you hear the alarm go off just gently find your way back to consciousness. After a while you will get quite used to programming yourself to allow your unconscious mind to tell you when it is time to come out of trance without the use of the clock.

One to Eight Progressive Relaxation Self-Hypnosis Induction (Script)

Placing myself in this comfortable position...I can allow my mind to take care of my body...**AS I CLOSE MY EYES I CAN GO INSIDE AND IMAGINE**...in my mind's eye I can see my favourite colour for deep relaxation...focusing on that colour it can grow...**LETTING THAT RELAXING COLOUR FILL THE BACK OF MY HEAD AND SHOULDERS**...**ONE**...**NOW!**...each bone... nerve...tissue...and muscle can give in to this progressive relaxation...and should I need to wake up I can...**HOWEVER FOR THIS TIME I CAN LET GO AND ENJOY MY INNER SELF**...the colour and even sound of deep relaxation can spread and flow...spreading through my face...eyes...jaw ...neck...shoulders...**SEEING AND FEELING RELAXATION PROGRESS COMFORTABLY**...**TWO**...**NOW!**...checking my mouth is open and that the airways are clear...the relaxation flowing down my arms...fingers...those good feelings can travel...**IGNORING THE WORLD OUTSIDE MY HEAD FOR A TIME**...allowing peace...calm...inner exploration...healing...and pure enjoyment...good feelings taking over my body...**LETTING THAT RELAXING COLOUR**...**SOUND**...**AND FEELING PROGRESS MORE**...**THREE**...**NOW!**... letting the part that knows how to take care of me do its job...each breath I breathe in can be full of deep relaxation...**BEING AWARE THAT NATURE KNOWS WHAT TO DO**...my chest...back...lumber region...bottom can all enjoy...giving into the flow of deep relaxation...**BECOMING AWARE OF MY BODY CHANGING**...**FOUR**...**NOW!**...as my breathing slows right down my body can sleep...resting...calmer...more peaceful...giving time to myself...**I AM BECOMING THE CENTRE OF MY UNIVERSE**...focusing on my tummy where my energy starts from as I eat...the experience of deep relaxation can be released...**SPREADING OUTWARDS LIKE A RIPPLE FROM THAT AREA**...**FIVE**...**NOW!**...this special time I deserve by the right that I exist...I am the principle being of my universe...**AS I FEEL GOOD THE WORLD AROUND ME SEEMS TO BECOME MORE POSITIVE**...all through my hips and the upper half of my body...the enjoyment of deep relaxation can spread...**MORE RELAXED WITH THOSE GOOD COLOURS**...**SOUNDS ...AND FEELINGS**...**SIX**...**NOW!**...this is a time for me to be in touch with my unconscious...as my conscious mind goes on holiday until I wake up...**LETTING MY GOOD FEELINGS SPREAD AND FLOW AND SPREAD AND FLOW**...progressing down my legs the relaxation can take me into a deep trance...any undue stress can go out off into the distance on the out breath...**MY BODY FEELING MORE AND MORE DEEPLY RELAXED ...SEVEN**...**NOW!**...my big toes and little toes can finally complete my transition...allowing the whole of my body to deeply relax...**I CAN LET NATURE TAKE ITS COURSE**...turning the colour into a cloud too and lying on it...so deeply relaxed my body can allow me peace...privacy...calm and comfort…***ALL THE WAY DOWN INTO A GOOD DEEP HYPNOTIC TRANCE …EIGHT…NOW!***

Some people ask if they go into a trance whether there is ever a time when they will not wake up. The answer is no, because trance eventually develops into natural sleep if the person does not wake up. Trance is a natural occurrence that happens to us all the time and hypnosis is just a way of utilising those trance processes. Be sure when you are composing trance scripts on tape that you include the coming out of trance script that follows to bring you back to wakefulness.

Visualisation

Many people ask what is **VISUALISATION** and can I do it? The fact is you do it all the time by imagining pictures inside your mind. When you think about what has, might or will happen you are imagining pictures inside your head of various scenes. You may not always be aware consciously that you are doing that but this is a natural process that happens all the time. What you can do is be aware of it happening and learn how to harness the process with your eyes closed and even with your eyes open.

Whether the pictures are black and white, colour or psychedelic is not important at this stage – just get used to being aware of your visualisations. Learn to draw, paint, and create pictures by any means you can inside your head. It can be still pictures or movies and as time passes you will become a more accomplished visualiser with control over the process, making it work for you.

Visualisation is one of the most powerful kinds of human motivation used by hypnotists, spiritual leaders, healers, and yogis for thousands of years. As time progresses you will learn to picture whatever you want in your mind and change its colour, speed of action, texture, contrast and all the constituents that make up those pictures. You can visualise your experience of trance inside your head as you go into, remain in and come out of a trance.

Imagery

When we talk about imagery we mean the different representations of our internal imagined experiences. You can also change the different experiences of visualisation, sound, feelings, smell and taste as you imagine them. **REMEMBER**…because it is your mind you can make up your imagination any way you need, want or desire to suit your own requirements. You may have limited control over the outside world but inside your head you are Leonardo Da Vinci, Walt Disney, Mozart, Jane Austen, Shakespeare or Margo Fonteyn.

There are two kinds of imagery which are called process and direct. Process imagery is a series of progressive images that can take you towards your goal of the ideal self in structured stages. It is as if you were going through a film in slow motion, experiencing each frame and understanding how to travel that journey from A to B.

Direct imagery is much faster and focused on the goal and going directly to it automatically. For some people or particular tasks it is all right to use direct imagery and allow your unconscious to guide you there directly. Neither type of imagery is superior so you can form it according to your own particular needs but what tends to happen is the more experienced you get at imagery the easier it is for you to use direct imagery. Of course we all need a story board from time to time and that is perfectly OK too. Remember...imagery, in all its sensory modes, is part of the trance process.

Brainwaves

There are five basic kinds of brainwave activity which are High Beta, Beta, Alpha, Theta and Delta. Using an EEG we can monitor the brain to show that during states of high anxiety the brainwaves are fast and show the High Beta state. Beta is the normal waking state. Alpha and Theta are where trance and deeper trance take place respectively. Very slow Delta wave activity is when a person is asleep. Along with the trance state, prayer, meditation and catalepsy can also take place in the Alpha and deeper Theta state.

High Beta = High activity mental state, including an anxiety attack, 23-35 cycles per second (cps).

Beta = The general alert state, 15-22cps.

Alpha = Relaxed, engaged in introspective (focusing inwards) activity (trance), 8-14cps.

Theta = Present in moments of deep insight/recalling vivid memory (deep trance), 5-7cps.

Delta = Deep sleep state, 0.5-4cps.

Alpha waves are what I would like you to encourage as you go into trance, creating and sensing deep relaxation, peace and calmness. The brain learns so easily when in Alpha waves, because the pathways are open to the unconscious. After all, we already have many of the resources we need to get through life happily, it is just that most of us have sometimes forgotten that we have them.

By encountering the state of Alpha wave production as we go into trance it enables us to once again be aware of all our own natural and learned resources. Around 20 to 30 minutes a day will make all the difference to the quality of your life, as while in trance, your unconscious rebalances your psyche and body, lowering your heart rate, regulating your cholesterol level and processing stress factors.

We often become so engaged with the outside world that we forget to pay attention to our own needs. As small children we started our learning experiences by first of all seeing ourselves as the centre of the universe which enables us to learn how to negotiate the world on our own terms. As adults the rigours of life can leave us not paying enough care and attention to our own health, welfare and happiness. The following script is designed to help you re-engage with yourself and find the centre of your being from which to face the world on your own terms.

REMEMBER...first record a trance induction...then use this script to cause change or have an experience in trance...and finish with a coming-out-of-trance script.

Finding My Centre (Script)

Being aware of myself I can see that sometimes I need to adjust...the living process can at times throw me out of balance with nature...***BECOMING AWARE OF MY OWN CENTRE CAN CONNECT ME TO THE EARTH THAT GIVES ME STRENGTH***...as I experience life as a journey...with its natural twisting hills and valleys...***I CAN SPEND THIS TIME JUST BEING***...I give myself the luxury of time that allows me to find my life feet again...and the gravity that keeps me grounded supports me...***I ACCEPT MY BODY IN MY MIND AND FIND MY CENTRE***...feeling my inner body I allow it to find its own equilibrium...the journey as well as the arrival gives me great pleasure and strength...***LETTING MY INNER PSYCHE GUIDE ME I TRUST IN NATURE***...millions of years of human development have led me to my body and mind...I can free myself by being apart from the outside world for a time...***SURRENDERING TO MY INNER SELF MY CENTRED FEELING CON-NECTS ME TO THE POWER OF THE PLANET'S FORCES***...I do not have to consciously understand the ways in which I balance myself...my uncon-scious knows exactly how to take care of me...***I CAN EVEN FLOAT FREE OF THE OUTSIDE WORLD***...my mind finds the centre of my body...this in turn can reconnect me to my inner resources...***ALLOWING MYSELF TO FIND MY CENTRE IN RELATION TO MY LIFE***...in my sleeping and waking life this will help me be a more balanced person...I will help others be more balanced too...***I AM CENTRING MYSELF AND ENJOYING COMING INTO MYSELF NATURALLY BALANCED...LETTING IT HAPPEN...NOW!***

Using all the senses in your imagination can help you create your own inner realities of sound, sight, touch, feeling, smell and taste. Each of these senses you can change in strength, tenacity, breadth, and context so that you have the experience that is right for you. Every time you go into a trance take con-trol of those senses and become more aware you can change your inner expe-riences which in turn also changes your outer experiences as you interact with the world.

You are creating your own virtual reality that allows you a special access to your natural resources. It also allows you to find out more about yourself and the strengths you possess. What is really important though is that hypnosis and trance allow you to practise your actions inside your head before you try them out in the real world.

To make an analogy, I have a friend who is an airline pilot and has been flying aeroplanes for 40 years. She recently decided not to do long haul Trans-Atlantic flights anymore because she wanted to be closer to home. In order for her to retrain to shorter runs in smaller aeroplanes in Europe she had to spend many hours in a simulator that gave her a virtual reality experience of flying those aeroplanes before she ever stepped into one.

So your mind is a place where you can paint the life you want onto a blank canvas and rehearse how to live out that life in full colour, sound, feelings, smell and taste. Your mind is housed in your brain which is the most complicated and original mechanism we know about that can be trusted to find ways forward for you.

Coming out of Trance (Script)

My time in trance has been a good experience...and I can spend other times in trance as well...***SLOWLY...GENTLY...BRINGING GOOD FEELINGS BACK WITH ME I CAN BEGIN TO WAKE UP...EIGHT***...it has been good to spend time with myself...exploring my inner world...***BRINGING BACK KNOWLEDGE TO MY WAKING LIFE...SEVEN***...feelings of calm...inner peace...and deep relaxation...having a deep sense of having rested inside and outside my body...***BEING MORE IN TUNE WITH MY NATURAL SELF...SIX***...enjoying being more prepared to face life in a balanced way...giving myself the time I deserve...and being loving and considerate to others too...***HALF AWAKE AND FINDING MYSELF MORE IN LOVE WITH LIFE...FIVE***...each day I can spend private time going into a trance...reinventing myself with every breath...***CREATING AND RECREATING MYSELF IN MANY WONDERFUL WAYS***...knowing intuitively what are good ways to live my life...enjoying a continuing sense of self development and wellness...***REMEMBERING THE NUMBER ONE RULE OF LIFE...HAVE FUN...THREE***...no matter what I do in life I can excel to my personal best...this gives me a sense of how very special I really am...***SPECIALNESS OUTSIDE AND INSIDE MY BODY CAN SHINE...TWO... MORE AWAKE***...happily being aware that I can use all my resources...learning continually to be a happier self...***WIDE AWAKE***...eyes open...refreshed and wide awake...***ONE...AWAKE AND RELAXED***.

The Way of Peace

To each and every one of us peace may mean many different things although some of us share common experiences of some aspects of our culturally and personally defined ideas of peace. Since more than two thirds of the world's population now live in cities we are, to a large extent, often at war with nature. The blade of grass or wild flowers that grow up through the pavement are not seen as a celebration of spring for the townie but yet another irritation that threatens their ordered and artificially constructed environment. People who live in towns and cities are often not fully aware of the changing seasons until they are expressed through the countryside during travel to yet another artificially constructed environment.

To a large part, humanity is at war with its environment and even with itself as we live under a huge amount of pressure to conform to the clock and perfunctory routines. Animals in the wild roam free, eat when they wish and generally sleep when they are tired. Humans, however, have been too successful in their breeding to afford the individual the freedom our ancestors naturally took for granted. Although we live longer with the help of modern medicine and science, the quality of that life is often substandard, and people suffering from depression believe they are forced to live in unnecessary misery.

With the arrival of the global society, people chase work that often leads them away from their families, roots and sociocultural support networks that we used to rely on. Loneliness plagues the modern world as people look for consolidation in consumerism and substance abuse.

Established religion and politics lose their dignity as tales of corruption fill the newspapers and television documentaries expose scandals covered up by our supposed mentors. So many people are turning back to paganism which offers a closer connection to nature and personal choice in the icons they create for themselves that are less likely to be destroyed by the vagaries of media paranoia.

LOOK WITHIN

We have come full circle as we rediscover that self-empowerment, security and hope arise not from the treadmill of the third millennium's consumerism but from the very places old philosophies taught us, though be it in different ways. Buddhism, Christianity, Islam, Hinduism and Taoism all told us to look within. Those religions often lost their way with constructed hierarchies that bid us pay homage to far-removed godlike figures, so now many of us have to make personal quests to find new strength from within.

The vast majority of us were brought up by half-hearted religious instruction that failed to give us the whole picture we could use to comfortably navigate the plains and rocky mountains of life. Our education filled us with maths, sciences, and foreign languages, but rarely prepared us for the game of survival or the ability to travel a spiritual quest.

It does not matter what religion you are, if any, there is a part of you that is the inexplicable essence of life that comes into your body at birth and leaves with your last dying breath. This is the part of us that comes forward in our awareness when we experience that ecstatic thing we call peace...whatever form it manifests in you.

This experience of peace and deep-seated calmness is so alien to so many people in this age that war fills our lives, not only between countries, towns, and religious groups, but also between the different parts of our own bodies and minds. Illness is a war in the body along with depression, feelings of loneliness and abandonment, helplessness, disappointment, anger and an ever present sense of hopelessness.

Since we cannot rely on other people to find the peace we seek then the only other choice we have is to create it for ourselves. Some people spend their whole lives seeking the illusion of peace, believing that it is elsewhere other than where they are at the present time so they keep on looking and despair in their search.

Imagination is the key that transcends reality and is limitless. It permits us to create and recreate whatever we like within our own mind. If you are relying on others to provide the peace that you need now and during your last breaths you will be waiting a long time. Peace can rest within you, but more importantly, peace begins its creation within you. The enemy of time for many people prevents them dedicating enough minutes in the day to look within and reinforce their understanding that whatever you want to experience can start from inside, moving outwards.

FROM THE INSIDE OUTWARDS

These words I write are not only for the poorest and most wretched among us but for the poorest and most wretched parts of each of us that we have ignored and neglected as life has overwhelmed us with its momentum. The only magic pills are the ones we create for ourselves. So allow yourself to **BE A MAGICIAN INSIDE YOUR HEAD**...leaving restrictions and the outside world behind. Put your body in a safe place and leave it there while you travel deep inside yourself.

In learning self-hypnosis you can bring together different scripts, after having gone into trance, one after the other during a single trance experience to give that trance many dimensions and purposes. Each single script can have a specific purpose and a combination of scripts joined together can take you into trance, letting you experience different trains of thoughts, actions, installing new programmes, wiping out unwanted ones, and bringing you back out of trance to the waking state.

The Way of Peace (Script)

Through life I have had many triumphs...sometimes pitfalls and hard knocks have been unpleasant...*I CAN CHOOSE HERE TO TAKE MY OWN PATH AND WAY OF PEACE*...there are countless temptations that beckon me to be egocentric...life offers me opportunities to remain angry...*BUT TAKING A PATH OF PEACE GIVES ME GREATER FREEDOM*...that does not mean being a victim...nor does it mean allowing people to take advantage of my good nature...***MY GOOD NATURE HOWEVER CAN KEEP REPRODUCING ITSELF***...looking around I can see that the world has many conflicts...it is true that many people are afraid of being crushed...***SO I WILL TAKE A LEAD BY LEARNING MORE ABOUT TAKING WAYS OF PEACE AS MY JOURNEY***...I recognise that life can sometimes be frustrating ...and that can be my signal to be creative in what I do...***LEAVING A BETTER WORLD BEHIND ME IS IMPORTANT TO ME***...like learning to walk a tightrope I can strike a balance...seeking a place between accommodating others and valuing my self-esteem...***I CAN MAKE MYSELF MORE DIFFERENT FROM THIS POINT ON***...as I imagine what it would be like to come back to this world again...I can see...hear...feel...taste and smell the legacy I have left for myself and others...***MY CAREFUL CONCLUSION THEN CAN BE THE WAY OF PEACE I IMPLEMENT HERE AND NOW!***

Installing Thoughts and Actions through Mantras in Self-Hypnosis

A mantra is a repetitious incantation used to induce an altered state of mind. Classically from Hinduism, it is any part of the Vedic literature which consists of metrical psalms of praise. The words become sacred and symbols are used along with them as objects of concentration. They can become instruments and the embodiment aspects of spiritual power; in Sanskrit a mantra means speech that is an instrument of thought.

Continuous words or thoughts indoctrinate the individual into an unconscious reflex reaction as learning behaviour takes place in four separate stages:

1. Unconsciously incompetent
2. Consciously incompetent
3. Consciously competent
4. Unconsciously competent

Mantras can be used in self-hypnosis to change actions and reflex reactions through self-suggestion. After continuous repetition the individual will find that they are reacting in different ways to situations, other people and the self, due to the use of intra-hypnotic and post-hypnotic suggestion. Behavioural alteration through positive mental programming and reinforcement using a mantra is an effective and elegant form of personal therapy.

Make up your own mantra of several words in the first person singular and present tense that tells your inner self that you have...**GREAT ABILITY TO PRACTISE SELF-HYPNOSIS**...and how you can create **INNER PEACE FROM INSIDE OUTWARDS**. Use this mantra when going into a trance.

Summary

■ Creating yourself from the inside outwards using your imagination to be and experience anything you need, want or desire – imagination is the key.

■ Appreciating life has active and resting stages, taking time to take time out.

■ Turning whatever happens in life into a learning experience from which you can draw knowledge. Using self-hypnosis to create and recreate yourself.

■ Going inside your mind to experience the trance-like state, trusting your unconscious to teach you what to do and keep you safe.

■ Understanding the structure of hypnotic scripts with three dots for three long seconds of rest, bold print for emphasis and paying attention to the six pointers for self-hypnosis.

■ Tape recording the induction at the beginning of your trance, including additional scripts for the middle of the trance and using the awakening script at the end.

■ Memorising each script and practising self-hypnosis without the tape after one week.

■ Bring your attention back into yourself by finding your centre, enabling you to focus on your life.

■ Discovering the way of peace, putting aside conflict, as the path to all things good.

■ Devising and installing your own mantras, both in trance and to be used consciously whenever you need them.

■ Do the exercise on p156.

Frequently Asked Questions

Q. What if I can't go into a trance?
A. You go into a trance all the time naturally throughout your life. Self-hypnosis is self-inducing those trances. Practise...practise...practise...so just close your eyes, go inside and think about it.

Q. Does it get easier as time goes on?
A. For some people they go into a trance on the first attempt. Others very soon after starting, and everyone finds that it not only gets easier but also automatic as you learn cues to take you straight into the trance state on command.

Q. Does it matter if I just stay listening to the tapes I make?
A. The tapes you make are a learning experience. As you learn to do self-hypnosis without the tapes then you are doing hypnosis in action which means you are gaining control over the process of your mind. The tapes are meant to be a week-long learning experience that are designed to teach you and not to be relied on in the long run. In many ways they are teaching you to kick start parts of your psyche you have not been using.

Q. I have heard that people can go into trances and never come out.
A. When you go into a trance you generally come back to consciousness when you awaken. If you awaken and think you are still in a trance then you could be in a state of artificial somnambulism which is being in a trance but seeming

awake. Even in this state you can count yourself out of trance by using the reverse number technique or your own special way of coming out of trance.

Q. Sometimes I begin to panic as I lose conscious control and go into a trance.
A. That is common for some people who have not been used to trusting their unconscious. Remember it is your unconscious mind that takes care of you when you are asleep and it does the same when you are in a trance. In other words it knows how to do its job and you can learn to trust it to do what it knows how to do.

Q. How many trance scripts can I use at once and how many times can I use them?
A. After having your basic going into and coming out of trance script you can put as many of the other scripts in between as you wish. Try to keep the trance to around half an hour, leaving a few minutes gap between each script for your mind and body to rest, process and be creative. Remember to pay attention to your timing, taking it slowly, allowing for the long three-second rests in the scripts, symbolised by three dots and not rushing your delivery.
Some scripts you may only ever need to use once or a couple of times and others you can use for days, weeks or months. When I am installing new programmes in my mind I might only use a script a couple of times until its results are effective. The script for strengthening my immune system (chapter eight) I use every day of my life.

Further Reading

ALMAN, BRIAN M & LAMBROU, PETER, **SELF-HYPNOSIS: THE COMPLETE MANUAL FOR HEALTH AND SELF-CHANGE**, BRUNNER/MAZEL PUBLISHERS, NEW YORK, 1983.

BANDLER, RICHARD & GRINDER, JOHN, **TRANCE-FORMATIONS: NEURO-LINGUISTIC PROGRAMMING AND THE STRUCTURE OF HYPNOSIS**, REAL PEOPLE PRESS, UTAH, USA, 1981.

BANDLER, RICHARD & MACDONALD, WILL, **AN INSIDER'S GUIDE TO SUB-MODALITIES**, META PUBLICATIONS, CA, USA, 1988.

CARRINGTON, PATRICIA, **THE BOOK OF MEDITATION**, ELEMENT BOOKS, DORSET, UK, 1977.

DEVANANDA, SWAMI VISHNU, **MEDITATION AND MANTRAS**, OM LOTUS PUBLISHING, NEW YORK, 1978.

FEZLER, WILLIAM, **CREATIVE IMAGERY: HOW TO VISUALISE IN ALL**

FIVE SENSES, FIRESIDE, NEW YORK, 1989.

GAWAIN, SHAKTI, **CREATIVE VISUALIZATION**, BANTAM BOOKS, NEW YORK, 1982.

HIRSHBERG, CARYLE & BARASCH, MARC IAN, **REMARKABLE RECOVERY**, RIVERHEAD BOOKS, NEW YORK, USA, 1995.

WOLINSKY, STEPHEN, PhD, **TRANCES PEOPLE LIVE: HEALING APPROACHES IN QUANTUM PSYCHOLOGY**, THE BRAMBLE COMPANY, USA, 1991.

Chapter Two

More About Self-Hypnosis

I want you to know that self-hypnosis is one of the strongest and most successful mind disciplines that you will come across that can help you have an extremely high quality of life experience. It will give you the control to be able to explore your own mind in a safe way as well as teaching you how to continually have the ability to programme and reprogramme your mind, body and emotions.

It does not matter if you are rich or poor, this work is about the quality of people's life experience and not a training manual to make someone a millionaire. Of course if that is what you want from life, the skills you learn here would certainly set you on the right road. From the many people I have helped over the years, some rich and some poor, I have become aware that money is in no way any kind of guarantee against unhappiness. What is a guarantee against unhappiness, however, is taking control of your own life and mind, and this is the empowerment that self-hypnosis gives you.

Each day of your life can be lived as if it is your very last so that the last day you ever live is a good day to live or die. None of us can cheat death when it is our turn but we all too often cheat ourselves of the life we could have had. It is never too late to have the kind of life you could call rewarding...right now...so go for it!

Overcoming the Fear of Losing Conscious Control

When I go out and give public talks to groups about hypnosis I often encounter people who have a set of preconceived notions that hypnosis is in some way controlling and dangerous. These are always people who are misinformed or afraid of losing conscious control and they may have other issues around how they are afraid of many other things in the world too. There may also be a large degree of inflexibility in their personality where they believe in narrow and restricted philosophies or ways of thinking.

To be fair to those people, hypnosis has had some bad press at times which misinforms people about how it works, what it is used for, and who is qualified to use it. The worst publicity for hypnosis comes from stage hypnotists. The majority of therapeutic professional organisations do not allow them to be members. Many of these stage hypnotists also end up damaging the people they hypnotise on the stage. But let me ask you to consider that if a circus knife thrower set themselves up as a surgeon, would you equally and rightfully have mistrust in them too?

Hypnosis is safe when used by a professionally qualified and recognised hypnotherapist. However, many doctors are so misinformed about hypnosis that they can often give their patients completely the wrong idea about how effective and efficient it can be in developing the mind.

When you use self-hypnosis under the guidance of this publication no one else is controlling your behaviour but yourself. The wonderful thing is that you are able to control your own behaviour, thoughts, physical body and emotions in ways you may not have been able to do before. That self-control and ability to explore the many resources you innately possess is very self-empowering and a great personal adventure of the kind that many people only ever dream about.

Inside your mind is a part of you that looks out for your personal safety. This is a part that operates automatically without your conscious awareness and sometimes it brings something to your conscious awareness in order for you to deal with it consciously. The more you trust and invest in that protective part doing its job automatically the more you are able to free up the capacity of your mind to explore what extraordinary abilities you actually possess.

When you give up conscious control during hypnosis you are allowing the larger part of your mind, which is the unconscious, to have a clear path to spring into action and perform whatever task needs to be done. Remember your conscious mind is less than 1 per cent of your whole mental abilities and the rest is your unconscious. Just think about that potential for a moment.

The progressive relaxation self-induction that you learnt earlier is a good way to go into trance but there are thousands more, so you can have the fun and variety of more inductions. Some people become afraid that they will not wake up from a trance. Remember you can always count yourself out of a trance backwards from **EIGHT TO ONE** suggesting to yourself that you can be...**WIDE AWAKE AND ALERT**...**WIDE AWAKE AND ALERT**.

Having been in a trance by a progressive method that is composed of numbered stages you can then go back into a trance very quickly by assuming the trance position again and counting those numbers. This allows you to re-experience that trance state again, letting go of the outside world as your mind and body recognise the trance state.

The Tumbling Trance Induction (Script)

Finding a safe and private place to rest my body with my head supported ...checking my limbs are uncrossed my breathing can become more relaxed...***KEEPING MY EYELIDS CLOSED I CAN ROLL MY EYEBALLS BACK OVER THE TOP OF MY HEAD***...letting go of everything in the outside world I can feel my inner body tumbling backwards...I can enjoy the freefalling backwards feeling of this trance induction...***THE MORE I TUMBLE BACKWARDS THE DEEPER I GO INTO A TRANCE***...experiencing absolute freedom of inner body movement...magically my cares can be left behind as like Alice I fall into Wonderland...***TUMBLING...TUMBLING***...

DEEPER AND DEEPER INTO A TRANCE OF ABSOLUTE FREEDOM...the tethers to reality can be severed for a while as I open my limbs in my mind...tumbling freely through space like a parachuting skydiver...**I CAN TUMBLE BACKWARDS INTO A BEAUTIFUL DEEP TRANCE ANYWHERE INSIDE I WOULD LIKE TO BE**...devoid of the laws of gravity I can be free inside my mind...free unconsciously to enjoy exploring my inside mind...**I CAN BE FREE TO EXPERIENCE A BEAUTIFUL FEELING OF FLOATING IN A TRANCE**...**NOW!**

The Colour Tunnel Induction (Script)

Colour is a wonderful medium for my inner mind to imagine with my eyes closed...as I travel into a tunnel the colours and experiences can change...**I CAN RECOGNISE THE FIRST STATE AS RED**...as I go deeper into the tunnel my body can relax more...my conscious mind can leave me at the entrance of the tunnel...**I CAN RECOGNISE THE JOURNEY AS GOING INTO A TRANCE**...travelling inwards towards my centre it is possible to see the colour changing...as the colour changes so do my experiences...**I CAN RECOGNISE THE COLOUR STATE OF ORANGE**...**WARMTH**...**LIKE ROBES OF BUDDHIST MONKS**...**MORE PEACEFUL**...deeper into the safety of my internal world I can travel...the tunnel opens up as I am learning the space is bigger inside than out...**I RECOGNISE THE COLOUR STATE OF YELLOW**...**COMMUNICATION INSIDE AND OUT**...deeper into trance I travel as the colours change...sounds...feelings...smells...tastes...thoughts...emotions can all change as well...**I RECOGNISE THE COLOUR STATE OF GREEN**...**NATURE**...**GROWTH**...**BIRTH**...**REBIRTH**...the more I travel inside myself the greater my understanding of my enormous human potential...leaving my body behind my mind takes me deeper...and deeper...**I RECOGNISE THE DEEP INNER BLUE TRANCE STATE FOR RESTING**...**RECOVERING**...**HEALING**...I give over the control of self-hypnosis to my inner unconscious mind...knowing the way it can take me deeper into trance...**I RECOGNISE THE INNER INDIGO STATE OF TRANCE THAT REPRESENTS LIFE ENERGY**...becoming aware that I am in a deep trance it is good to allow my mind to teach me what incredible resources I truly have...being able to take many of those resources with me back to my waking life...**I CAN RECOGNISE THE INNER TRANCE PURPLE STATE OF SUCCESS**...**MY SUCCESS**...**MY ROYAL SELF**...with my body totally relaxed in my inner mind I can allow the colours to find their own way...my private inner world safe away from any distractions...**I CAN RECOGNISE THE INNER STATE OF DEEP TRANCE**...**SAFETY**...**CALM**...**PEACEFUL**...**AN OPEN PALLET FOR MY IMAGINATION TO PAINT ANYTHING IT WANTS**...

Deepening a Trance

There are many reasons to deepen a trance once you are in a trance although some of the work you do on yourself may be just as effective in the light trance state. You may want to be in a deep trance to experience intense rest, deep mental reprogramming, dealing with material that the conscious mind cannot handle, solution-focused hypnotic dreaming, or anaesthesia and analgesia. For some of these you will benefit from a visit to a hypnotherapist to help you gain your skills quickly and confidently.

Stairs Deepener (To be used after a normal induction script)

Since I am resting comfortably in a trance I can understand my unconscious mind guides me...leaving my body further behind I can go deeper into the inner mind...***AT THE TOP OF A VERY GRAND STAIRCASE I CAN BEGIN TO WALK DOWNWARDS***...each step down can take me deeper...all the way down into a more peaceful...relaxing place...***DESCENDING***...***NINE***...***10***...***11***...***12***...***13***...***14***...***15***...***16***...comfortably allowing my unconscious mind to take care of my body as I go deeper inside...giving myself over to the absolute experience of living in my inner mind...***IN A PROFOUND TRANCE***...***HYPNOTICALLY ASLEEP.***

Lift and Escalator Deepener

One of the psychoimaginary images that a lot of people use to take them deeper faster is that of a lift or escalator. This is one that I use myself once I am down in a trance and as I step into the lift I press buttons with different letters on them to express me down into a profound trance. One of the things you need to remember is that when you are ready to come out of the trance you need to come back up in the lift or take the stairs in reverse to normal trance depth before you count yourself out of trance.

I want you to try this technique but I am not going to give you any further instruction because I just want you to make up your own imagery as you experience the fun and empowerment of becoming your own self-hypnotherapist.

The Use of Music for Inductions

Have you ever listened to a piece of music that has just transported you somewhere else instantly? It changed your mindset, emotions, level of functioning, internal feelings and pictures. In other words it sends you into a trance. There are certain pieces of music that send me to somewhere other than consciousness but for everyone those pieces of music may be different.

Early Baroque music and modern pieces that are set at 60 beats a minute can have the effect of changing your brainwaves to take you into the Alpha state, which as you know is the brainwave activity associated with the trance state. There have been a range of such pieces composed by many new age musicians that can be bought in alternative health shops. Your favourite classical music can have the same effect but not pieces that are thunderous or likely to take you into the High Beta state of alarm.

Many composers understand that certain musical beats, cords and arrangements can have this effect on mental functioning and compose their music accordingly. Some classical compositions are perfect examples of pieces of music that were composed to send people to sleep, often commissioned to cure insomnia.

Rock music will not do this as it over-stimulates the brain and sends the person into High Beta wave activity. Neither will pieces like the *1812 Overture* or Beethoven's *9th Symphony*. Look on the covers of the tape or disc containers or ask the shop assistant because new age music is often marked to tell you if it induces Alpha or Theta brainwaves for trance.

Learn the music, place your body in a safe place with your eyes closed, and associate it with putting yourself in the relaxed trance state so each time you imagine that music inside your head you are able to take yourself into a trance state.

The sound of crickets has the same effect on me as for years when I used to go to my house in the country it was the place where I always slept the best. As soon as I heard those crickets I would just want to lie down and sleep. Having made the association between a particular kind of soothing music or natural sounds, like the running of a stream, and the trance state, you can find that when you play that music or sound, or imagine it, you will go into a trance.

Induction through Sound and Light Machines

For the past dozen years there have been a selection of machines which have come onto the market that help induce particular brainwave patterns. The early models only involved headphones that emitted a series of clicking sounds known as binaural beats which changed their frequency over a period of minutes to take the person's brain down into the Alpha or Theta state.

Later came the machines with flashing light goggles added that are more effective at state induction because they use the two sensory systems of sound and sight. Experiments have shown that these machines are good at inducing certain brainwave states and there is also a facility where you can play sound recordings through the headphones at the same time.

While these machines are lots of fun and very good at inducing Alpha brainwave activity the trances they induce are passive and for much of the work in these pages you will need to be inducing active trances where you still have a lot of control over your thoughts and programming.

The Use of Pre-Recorded Tapes

As a professional hypnotist and therapist I have to tell you that I do not approve of the use of pre-recorded tapes sold on a commercial basis. Some professional therapists believe that it is unethical to try to develop everyone's mind by the same method or induction because everyone is different and the success rate will be limited. Where then does it leave the people for whom the tape did not work?

Moreover, we consider some such tapes to be dangerous because they often hold hidden subliminal messages that cannot be heard by the conscious ear, which betrays the trust of the person listening to them. Each tape needs to be made and tailored to an individual and only that way can it be effective and totally safe for them to use. If you are making the tape for yourself or a hypnotist is making a tape specially for you alone, then that is fine.

Safe Place Imagery

Sometimes the unconscious mind throws up material that can be too uncomfortable to be dealt with by the conscious mind. There are also other times when a person simply wants to go to a place that is comfortable, familiar and safe. If you have imagery or hallucinations that constantly trouble you or are coming up during hypnosis that are too difficult for you to deal with, consult a well qualified hypnotherapist for help.

Safe Place Imagery (Script)

There is a place I can go to that is my sanctuary...far...far away this place can offer me comfort...***I CAN CALL THIS MY SAFE PLACE***...it may be mountains or beaches or a garden or anywhere I feel safe...secure...and pleasantly surrounded...it is possible to go to this place in my mind anytime I want to....***I CAN DECIDE HOW THIS PLACE IS IN MY MIND***...yet this place can be altered at any time to add many wonderful things...here I can safely experience love...calm...tranquillity...peace...happiness...***I CAN BE SAFE FROM ANY UNPLEASANTNESS IN THIS WONDERFUL PLACE*** ...nothing can touch me here as this is a magic place known only to me...when I have been here I can feel rested...peaceful...and ready for life again...***I CAN GO TO MY SAFE PLACE BY SIMPLY RECITING IN MY MIND...SAFE PLACE...SAFE PLACE***...and it will come into my mind with the pictures...sounds and feelings that go with this safe place...***I CAN ENJOY THE FREEDOM MY SAFE PLACE GIVES ME ANYTIME I NEED ...WANT...OR DESIRE***.

Standard Habit Breaking and New Behaviour Installation

For simple habit eradication such as smoking, nail biting and hair pulling it is possible to reprogramme yourself without necessarily going into analysis to find out the root cause of the habit's origins. Obviously for more complicated addictions like alcoholism, single or multiple drug addictions it is necessary to consult a professional hypnotherapist, doctor, therapist, psychiatrist or psychologist.

Many habits are not only faulty thinking mechanisms but also an inability to deal with stress and tension. It is astounding the number of people walking around living their lives without strategies for dealing with unnecessary stress.

By breaking behaviour down into simple steps and then changing those steps individually, not only can you erase old behaviour, but you can also install new behaviour. The methods that we are going to concentrate on here are called cognitive **THOUGHT STOPPING** and **NEW BEHAVIOUR INSTALLATION**. As you break the technique into three easy stages, understanding each stage, then it is important to join them all back up again to make a complete and continuous flowing behavioural change as part of a larger trance script.

The three stages are:
1. Interrupting cues for the old behaviour
2. Breathing and releasing tension
3. Installing the new behaviour and creating good feelings

Stage 1 (Script)

I choose to no longer (name the old behaviour) and can clearly define that behaviour in my mind...seeing the sequences of my old behaviour playing through like a film...*I CAN VERBALISE EXTERNALLY WHAT THE BEHAVIOUR IS THAT I NO LONGER WANT* (and do just that)...each time I should find myself doing or about to do that old behaviour I can become aware it is happening...an alarm can go off in my head to alert me to that old behaviour...*I WILL HEAR THE WORD...STOP!...IN MY OWN VOICE INSIDE MY MIND*...it is possible for that alarm to activate also in other sensory systems...I can see an internal screen inside my head...*THE WORD ...STOP!...WILL ILLUMINATE IN BIG LETTERS INSIDE MY HEAD*...my body can also react to the alarm signal...whatever part of the body is engaged in the old behaviour will become inactive...*I WILL FEEL THAT PART OF MY BODY UNABLE TO DO THAT OLD BEHAVIOUR*.

Stage 2 (Script)

My lungs fill with three deep breaths...on each exhalation tension will leave my body...*TAKING A FIRST DEEP BREATH...HOLDING IT TIGHT INSIDE...RELEASING THE BREATH AND THE TENSION*...allowing the tension to leave my body with each out breath...taking the second deep breath and holding it tight inside me...*RELEASING FURTHER TENSION OFF ON THE SECOND DEEP OUT BREATH THAT LEAVES MY BODY*...*taking the third deep breath inside me and holding it...allowing the remaining tension to come into my body*...*THE REST OF THAT EXCESS TENSION CAN GO OFF INTO THE DISTANCE AS I EXHALE*.

Stage 3 (Script)

As I am becoming aware that I am not doing the old behaviour I can smile...letting all the good feelings of endorphins and seratonin go around my body enjoyably...***EXPERIENCING THOSE GOOD FEELINGS I CAN SUGGEST THE NEW REPLACEMENT BEHAVIOUR*** (name that behaviour) ***TO MYSELF NOW!***...with a clear mind I can continually suggest the new behaviour to myself...with those suggestions I can experience the good feelings allowing the two to become the same...***I CAN FEEL GOOD ABOUT THE NEW SUGGESTIONS THAT I AM MAKING TO MYSELF*** (state those suggestions)...as well as hearing those suggestions inside my head I can see them on a screen inside my mind...learning to recognise the good feelings that go with the new behaviour (state those suggestions)...***I CAN HEAR ...FEEL...AND SEE MYSELF PERFORMING THE NEW BEHAVIOUR NOW!***

Remember it is always important to state the new suggestion in a positive way about what you are doing and will do, and not to tell yourself what you will not do. Start the trance with the induction, go through each of the three stages, and close with a coming out of trance script. Record the whole trance experience onto a tape, using it three times a day for a week. Then learn every word of the whole script and recite it all to yourself inside your head as you continue making your own trance experiences twice a day without the tape. As the old behaviour disappears and the new behaviour becomes part of your daily life, repeat the trance every so often as a strengthener or refresher.

Dealing with Overwhelming Emotions

A lot of people find themselves swamped by overwhelming negative emotions that they feel they have no control over. There may be many kinds of emotions like loneliness, feelings of unworthiness, consumed with guilt about something they may have done years ago, rejection because a relationship did not work out, bereavement, sadness, unhappiness, anger, frustration, hopelessness. Some of these emotions may involve feelings not mentioned here or a combination of negative feelings, thoughts and emotions.

While it is natural to feel some negative emotions after something unpleasant has happened to you, because it is part of the natural assessment thinking processes that help you decide if you want to go there again, lingering negative emotions serve no purpose. They do, however, become a habit in some people who have not learned how to move on to the next stage of their lives. When negative emotions linger they become destructive and are turned in on the self, destroying well being.

Because your conscious mind is only very small and your unconscious mind is the greater part of you, it is logical to allow the unconscious mind to handle the resolution and change that you need while you are in a trance. Trust your unconscious mind because it contains all your life's learnings and your conscious mind only has a short attention span before it forgets what you are thinking about.

When using the following script, put it on a tape in the middle of an induction and an awakening but repeat the script several times during the trance.

Eliminating Negative Emotions (Script)

This can be a time for change at a deep unconscious level...I do not necessarily have to understand the changes consciously...***I CAN ALLOW MY CONSCIOUS MIND TO KNOW WHAT MY UNCONSCIOUS MIND CHOOSES TO DISCLOSE***...the negative emotions I have been experiencing were for a reason...it is possible to recognise that they too had a job to do in my life ...***BUT I CAN ALLOW MYSELF TO CHANGE AT A DEEP UNCONSCIOUS LEVEL***...whatever I have learned I can retain as knowledge...inside my mind I can see a magical conversion machine...***I CAN AND WILL ALLOW MY UNCONSCIOUS TO CONVERT THE NEGATIVE EMOTIONS INTO NEW POSITIVE ENERGY***...it is good to remember that I do not have to understand everything consciously...allowing the greater power of the unconscious to make that magical conversion...***I AM MAGNIFYING WHAT HAPPENS IN NATURE NATURALLY CONVERTING NEGATIVE EMOTIONS INTO A POSITIVE DIRECTION***...the thinking through of things can happen as my emotions begin to change...a brighter outlook will emerge as I begin to feel much better in myself...***I AM CHANGING ONCE AGAIN FROM THE INSIDE OUTWARDS***...seeing that magical conversion machine in my mind...negative emotions being eaten up and positive emotions coming out the other end...***I CAN ALLOW MY UNCONSCIOUS MIND TO NATURALLY PRODUCE MORE POSITIVE EMOTIONS THAT CHANGE THE WAY I THINK AND FEEL NOW!***

Negative thoughts always come with negative feelings and emotions so I would like you to do an exercise that will not only teach you to convert but will also begin to teach you to construct your own hypnotic suggestions. Recall a time when you were really low and write down what you were thinking, feeling and emotionally experiencing at the time. When you have done that, identify what the opposite of these experiences would be and write your own trance script to install those positive thoughts, feelings and emotions.

Also use the image of the conversion machine in your mind to convert negative thoughts into positive ones that can be constructive in your life and not destructive. Make lists of the two extremes to help you learn to identify the difference.

Being Aware of Surfacing Memories

One of the things that can begin to happen when you start to practise hypnosis is that memories from the past may come back to you which you have completely forgotten about. As I began self-hypnosis, one of the earliest memories that came to me was when I was sitting in my pram at nine months' old, trying to reach for my mother's chocolate on the sideboard. It was quite a surprise that memory came back to me so clearly because it was not something I have ever thought about consciously.

The funny thing is my mother does not remember such a thing ever happening. She is now 75 years old and often remembers things from the past as being quite different from how I remember them. Whether her memory or mine was the true one is not very important because all memories are actually false. When I say false I mean that we all construct our memories according to our own perspective and needs, so no two people will have exactly the same memory.

This is why hypnotically induced memories are generally not acceptable in court as being fully accurate as evidence, even though they may have been a precise representation of events. We also need to consider the way we reconstruct our memories of the past in the present as being largely dependent on what we may be needing from the present moment. Many therapists over the past 10 years have been sued for creating False Memory Syndrome (FMS) where they have been suggesting to their clients memories of abuse that never really happened.

I want you to be aware that if you have any abuse in your past there is a possibility that hypnosis may release memories of those events. There is also the grey area of pseudo-memories which can make a person unsure whether something was actually a real memory or a creation of their present day mind. It is important for all memories to always be treated as if they were real and dealt with seriously. If they were, however, to be acted on as proof that abuse did happen, they need to backed up by evidence. When in doubt, consult a well qualified therapist.

Trance Dreaming

Dreaming is a natural way for the mind to process information, work out solutions, permeate possibilities and simply have fun. We have all had times when we have been perplexed about a problem, gone to bed, and then woken up with the issues and solutions clarified in our minds. There have been other times when ideas have come to us during our sleep. Famous philosophers and scientists have had their very best ideas during dream-like states, just like Einstein and his theory of relativity.

Since we receive so many millions of pieces of information a day there is not enough time for us to fully process all of them so during sleep our minds catalogue, sort, process and deal with that information. We can have quite bizarre dreams as our mind presents us with thousands of different options and then selects an option that can be good for us. Without the bizarre dreams we would not be able to find the middle roads that are acceptable to our lifestyles.

Dreaming is truly a wonderful way of just letting our unconscious mind work through things in order to give us the best possible options. I have talked earlier about how big the unconscious mind is compared with the limited abilities of the conscious mind so does it not make sense just to allow yourself to dream your way forward?

A lot of people like to use this kind of script before they go to sleep at night to help them have healthy, active dreams during the sleep process.

Dreaming Trance (Script)

Sleep is a natural way of allowing the brain to work at its own pace...freeing the abilities of the unconscious mind...***I CAN THINK OF A PROBLEM TO WHICH I WOULD LIKE TO FIND A SOLUTION*** *(state the problem)*...my ability to dream is a natural way of thinking things through...not having to work out the solutions consciously...***I CAN ALLOW MYSELF TO DREAM DIFFERENT KINDS OF SOLUTIONS TO THAT SITUATION***...not having to choose one straight away...allowing myself the luxury of spending all the time I need inside my dreams...***I CAN BE AWARE OF MY PROFOUND DREAMING POTENTIAL***...totally relaxing my body as it goes to sleep... allowing my mind to dream comfortably with pleasure...***MY DREAM MERCHANTS CAN OFFER ME MANY DREAMS FROM WHICH TO CHOOSE***...in time my unconscious mind can let my conscious mind know the solutions...there is no rush...there is no hurry...***I CAN TAKE ALL THE TIME I NEED INSIDE MY HEAD***...and the funny thing is that the dreams I dream can be so creative...allowing me to enjoy them just for the pleasure of having them...***I DO NOT HAVE TO REMEMBER THOSE DREAMS CONSCIOUSLY***...my conscious mind can know what it needs to know in good time...slowly allowing myself to go into a hypnotic sleep and dream...***I CAN GO INTO A HYPNOTIC SLEEP AND DREAM NOW!*** *(five minute space)*

Summary

■ Learning to let go of conscious control and trusting your unconscious to be intelligent enough to take care of you and help you plot the best course forward in life.

■ Experimenting with inductions as you discover cues for instantly taking you into trance. Experiencing deeper states of trance that can be used for rest and rejuvenation along with deep seated reprogramming.

■ Installing your safe place imagery where you can go to whenever you need, want or desire sanctuary in trance or out, a place known only to you that can provide you with privacy, comfort and protection.

■ Simple habit breaking by using the thought and behaviour stopping technique. Installing new good behaviours along with good feelings and thoughts that go with those new mindsets and actions.

■ Dealing with overwhelming, swamping and negative emotions to convert them into positive energy that can be used to take you in a better direction and away from uncontrollable thoughts and states.

■ Putting surfacing memories into perspective as you learn to deal with the contents of your unconscious and be unafraid of asking for professional help should you need a helping hand.

■ Allowing yourself to experience trance dreaming and its uses to explore the possibilities for the future, creating new options at a deep unconscious level and simply enjoying the creativity of your dream time.

■ Do the exercises on p157 and p165.

Frequently Asked Questions

Q. Can I make up my own way of going into a trance?

A. Certainly and already you are a self-hypnotist using your imagination to take you where you want. Be sure of course to make up your own way of coming out of trance too.

Q. Is it good to analyse my dreams or the dreams I remember having during a trance session?

A. Lots of people profess to understand other people's dreams, although the real meaning of what goes on inside your head can be known only to you. We all actually experience the world according to our own physical, psychological and spiritual make-up so you can be sure your unconscious mind will let you know what it needs you to know at a time it needs you to know that. So you can have fun thinking and wondering about your dreams and what they might have meant.

Q. What if I wake up suddenly from a trance?

A. It means the trance has finished or been interrupted by an outside influence. You can simply carry on with your day or choose to go back into trance if you wish. Remember that you have put a command into your mind which will wake you up from trance and return you to normal wakefulness anytime it is necessary.

Q. What if I go into a trance and remain there for a long time beyond 30 minutes?

A. Your unconscious knows what it is doing so listen to what it is saying to you. Either you have work that the unconscious wants you to do in the longer trance state or you have fallen asleep because you are tired.

Q. Do I always have to spend 20 to 30 minues in trance?

A. Not necessarily. I often have what I call little booster mini-trances in the middle of a busy day. I may sit in my office and go inside to have a calming 10-minute trance to induce relaxation and rejuvenate my mind and body so that I am bright, alive and comfortable for the rest of the day. For me, energy starts with calm, never desperation.

Further Reading

HUXLEY, ALDOUS, **THE DOORS OF PERCEPTION**, HARPER COLLINS, LONDON, 1954.

JAMES, MURIEL & JONGEWARD, DOROTHY, **BORN TO WIN**, ADDISON WESLEY, NEW YORK, 1971.

JUNG, CG, **MEMORIES DREAMS & REFLECTIONS**, VINTAGE BOOKS, USA, JUNE, 1989.

Chapter Three

Owning Your Natural Potential

Although I am a hypnotist this is not a work about telling you, the reader, what to do; rather it is a piece of work in which I seek to share with you my belief in your inexhaustible abilities. I have observed that most people walk around with large parts of their brains metaphorically switched off. Einstein said that we only use 10 per cent of our brains, but I have to say I think he over-estimated. The way in which societies are structured turns a large percentage of people into partial automatons who do what, when, and where they are told, largely without question.

Let's face it, what would get done if everybody walked around thinking they were brilliant? Where would any country be with more leaders than voters? Who would pick up the garbage or sweep the streets?

Right from childhood many of us were programmed into being little robots who do nearly everything automatically without thinking about the long-term consequences of our actions. There are route systems where we go to school and maybe university, get a job, work for a ridiculous amount of years, form relationships according to accepted rules and then die in places designated for old people. Just occasionally we will rebel against something but generally we go through life with many of our reasoning processes on automatic. Don't believe a word I say – prove me wrong – watch the people around you.

After you have watched others, turn the spotlight on your own life and examine the behaviour patterns that you have set up to be automatic. Some of them will be very good for you like eating, bathing, rest and sex. Others will be faulty and you will find yourself doing things repeatedly that produce poor results.

So answer me this question…if you continually put your money into a savings account and that bank kept losing it, would you continue to invest with it?

Think of your behaviours as investments, life as the bank, and the dividends as the results you achieve. Are you gaining excellent returns from the behaviours you are investing? If not, then read on. But if all you want in life is episodes of sadness, unhappiness, pain, mediocrity, or to just be another sheep then this book is not for you; stop reading it, and give it to someone who wants excellence.

If you are continuing to read on, you are a genius, and even the person who has put it down is also a genius, but they have just not realised it yet. Think about it…your brain runs millions of cells in your body…co-ordinating them to form a human being…***ONLY A GENIUS COULD DO THAT…YES YOU!***

At school, children are marched off into graded categories according to statistical analysis, rarely developing the individual and helping a child tap into their natural abilities and genius. Shakespeare, Leonardo da Vinci, Michaelangelo, Mozart, Marie Curie, and Einstein are unlikely to have been such geniuses had they gone through the public school systems of today.

As you read this you can realise that your brain not only runs your body, but also your life, and it is possible to become aware that you can do anything you want. What you need to learn to do, however, is programme and reprogramme your mind in order to get yourself where you want to go...***AND HYPNOSIS IS THE FASTEST AND MOST EFFECTIVE WAY OF DOING THIS***.

The conscious mind is where many of the defence mechanisms reside that can object to any programming. When the conscious mind is out of the way or otherwise occupied during hypnosis, there is a direct inroad into the automatic programming routines that operate everything you do. Reprogramming in trance during hypnosis quickly sets up new behavioural routines and subroutines.

Many people turn up at my office telling me that they feel a failure and can never do anything right. So I teach them the ***NOW*** exercise that can be done without a formal induction script.

The *Now* Exercise (Script)

I can sit in a chair and be aware that my eyes can be comfortably closed ...letting the outside world go by without me for a time...***I CAN BRING MY FOCUS INTO THE PRESENT MOMENT BY THINKING I AM IN THE NOW***...I can become aware of my toes inside my shoes...of my fingers at the end of my hands...***AWARE OF BEING INSIDE MY OWN BODY***...the breath can come in my nose and out of my mouth...slowly breathing I can be aware of my lungs working....***MY INNER VOICE CONTINUALLY SAYING...NOW...AS I COME INTO THE PRESENT***...as each moment passes I can become more aware that I exist within my body...the sensation of the beating of my heart can tell me I am alive...***I EXIST HERE AND NOW***...it can be easier to distinguish where my clothes finish and where I begin...I am a living entity that is alive...***I AM AN UNDENIABLE SUCCESS AT BEING ALIVE***...as hard as I might try I cannot degrade the experience of my success at being alive ...I can be aware that I will always be a success at living during my whole life...***I CAN HAVE THIS SUCCESS NOW AND ALL MY LIFE***...from each experience I can learn...that knowledge can teach me how to approach things differently in future...***I CAN KNOW TAKING PART IN LIFE IS A MARK OF SUCCESS***.

Sometimes the very simplest logic can be used to flip us out of dysfunctional behavioural routines that detract from the good experience of well being and personal excellence. People do not generally stay in therapy with me very long as I see my job as trying to be made redundant as soon as possible. It is my sincere hope and belief that my clients can go away from therapy doing it for themselves. My first belief I have about anyone who enters my office is that those people will be able to do it themselves once they know how.

So with these exercises you are learning brain control, mind mechanics, realisation of your own abilities, plus how smart your mind and body are when they work together purposefully. You can have a realisation of your innate ability to be the kind of genius that can do anything you want to with your own life experience.

The Power of Self-Suggestion

Have you ever talked to yourself, seen in your mind something you might like to happen or heard your favourite calming music in your head? That's right...you have done all of those things, just as I have, because it is part of our natural mental processes. Self-suggestion is a powerful way to imprint and reimprint ideas on your mind so that they become part of your automatic thought mechanisms.

Whatever you want to happen to you in your life, get used to suggesting it to yourself. Visualise it happening, hear the sounds that go with it, listen to your own voice in your head telling you that it is happening or is going to happen. Then imagine how good you will feel when it has happened, remembering those good feelings, and then recall them when you want to make those imaginings translate into reality.

The *placebo effect* is when a person causes something to happen by processing a suggestion. If a doctor in a white coat gives you a pill and tells you it will cure your headache then it is often likely to cause that to happen even if the pill is only chalk. So it was not the pill that cured the headache, simply the belief in what the doctor told you and your belief in what doctors in white coats tell you.

The *negative placebo effect* can cause what may be good medicine not to work. If a doctor in white coat tells you that the medicine will not work it may not because psychology can override physiology.

Watch people's reactions in restaurants if you begin to throw up and say that the food is definitely off – but don't tell them I sent you.

So not only suggestions given by others but also self-suggestions are very strong drivers towards making behaviours happen, preventing them from happening and even changing physiology.

Truth and Suggestion

You may be wondering why the scripts that are being used are composed in the ways that they are. One of the general ways in which hypnotists make suggestions to people is to use two true statements and then a suggestion to follow. The suggestion is marked with particular emphasis like the statements in bold capitals in this work. What tends to happen is that the unconscious mind then accepts the third statement as being a truth as well. This principle also works during the self-hypnosis process.

What tends to happen is that because continual statements are being made, a backlog builds up and the mind tries to process all of them more quickly. For easiness' sake the mind follows a pattern of acceptance if it knows the previous statements to be true.

You can replace some of the true statements with further suggestions and because your mind is continually accepting information to process it quickly, it will be more comfortable in also accepting those extra suggestions.

Changing Your Beliefs

So many people are walking around with a set of outdated beliefs. I do not mean here that those beliefs are unfashionable, although they might be, but that they are beliefs which are no longer applicable to that person's present circumstances. As we change, due to our journey through life, there is a need for our beliefs to change as well.

Belief Changing (Script)

I can find myself in a cinema in my mind...it can be a very comfortable place as my body remains safe...*I CAN USE MY MIND TO INSTALL A GOOD BELIEF*...on the screen I can place one of my existing unshakeable beliefs...taking notice of its visual...sound...feeling...smell...and taste components...*I CAN BE AWARE OF THE STRONG ELEMENTS THAT MAKE THAT UNSHAKEABLE BELIEF WORK FOR ME*...by the side of the screen in my favourite neon colour I can list the elements that make that belief true...I can record the visuals...sounds...feelings and every component that makes that belief unshakeable...*I CAN BE AWARE I KNOW HOW TO HAVE AN UNSHAKEABLE BELIEF*...as I put that belief to one side leaving it completely intact I can bring the new desirable belief up on the screen...I can use the neon list of visuals...sounds...feelings...smells...tastes to install the new belief that will be strong for me...*AS I INSTALL THAT NEW BELIEF I MAKE IT A REALITY FOR ME*...taking all the time I need inside my head...I can fine tune the components of that new belief to make it real by using the neon list...*I CAN ALLOW THAT NEW BELIEF TO BECOME AS REAL AS THE OLD BELIEF NOW!*

The Use of Positive Affirmations

This is one of the most important lessons I teach to people because it helps them gain control of their situations and direct things to happen the way they want them to go.

When people who are in trouble come to see me they are always singing the same song. It might be a different tune for each person but the song is always

the same. The first line goes:
  Look what life has done to me.
The second line goes:
  It is happening to me and I don't have any control.
And the chorus sounds like:
  Help...Help...I need someone else to fix it for me.

This mode of operating is called **REACTIVE** and I am not judging anyone by pointing out the style of thinking and beliefs behind what they are doing in their minds to make and maintain their problems. I do, however, want you to analyse your thought patterns and behaviours, and begin to recognise when and if you are thinking this way.

Since I was born on the wrong side of the tracks myself, in poverty, sometimes homeless, and had very little education as a child this is exactly the kind of song I learnt to sing myself. Remember, however, when little orphan Annie sings it, it is cute but when 60-year-old Baby Jane sings the same old song it gets ridiculous.

To get to a different place you have to learn to sing a different kind of song, with different voices, say new things to yourself, create different pictures in your mind and very different feelings. The voices need to state **POSITIVE AFFIRMATIONS** about what you can achieve that motivate you towards your goals.

Those positive affirmations need to be stated in the **POSITIVE** about what you **CAN** and **WILL** do or **ARE** doing. This sets up the right neural pathways, values, beliefs, and attitudes to allow such actions to take place. As those actions then take place you are moving into the **ACTIVE** mode which will give you control over your life and situation. Learning to distinguish between *active* and *reactive* modes of operation is a key strategy to self-empowerment.

As I said earlier I would not advise anyone to state new suggestions in the negative like what you *don't, shouldn't, mustn't, won't, or can't* do. Such thinking will always set a person up for failure, as it is negative governing in hypnosis terms, and people tend eventually to rebel against what they are not supposed to be doing.

What makes positive affirmations really strong is when you bring them into the present tense in trance (intra-hypnotic suggestion) in the first person singular, for example:

I AM STRONG...NOW
I AM HEALING...NOW
I AM A GENIUS...NOW
I AM CONFIDENT...NOW
I AM ABLE TO RELAX...NOW
I AM GOING INTO A TRANCE...NOW
I HAVE CONTROL OVER MY BODY...NOW

Bringing self-affirmations into the present tense, in the first person singular, demands that the suggestion is translated into experience immediately. The mindsets (thinking structures) that process an action and experience become focused as you make your suggestions. Then your suggestions will operate the right neural pathways to allow the suggestion to become an action.

Discipline in the Mind

One of the most useful lessons that a parent or teacher can give to a child is to help them discipline their minds. The middle classes and wealthy spend their money instilling in their offspring a sense of continuity. Monastic and religious orders of all kinds place great value on grooming people's thought processes to be able to repeatedly apply themselves to a task or problem. I would go as far as to say that it is not the brilliant minded who run the world, simply the most persistent, who daily work away at achieving their goals.

Remember how as a child you learnt nursery rhymes and then later your numerical tables that started with two plus two equals four. Later came the reciting of poetry and recitation of prayers until you were able to remember scientific formulas and conjugated foreign language verbs.

When learning how to drive a car the beginner fumbles around, stumbling from mistake to mistake before they reach a level of competence that is eventually sufficient to enable them to pass their driving test. What were once a series of different steps then begin to be strung together to sequentially lead to automatic elegance of performance.

Different versions of the same kind of learning steps are used by the mind to continually pick up new tasks, skills and re-educate the brain into being able to surpass its earlier inability to perform.

Repetition of Thought

For most of us to get to a stage of competence from ignorance and inability takes a certain amount of repetition of process. Whether it is the programming of a physical or mental skill the same basic rules apply. Repetition of thought hardwires the brain into new kinds of thinking and behaviour patterns.

A baby tries to stand, continually falls down, and gets back up again until it is able to balance and judge the distance from one object to another without the assistance of the parents. It gets up time and time again as the brain forges new programming, learning to refine each stage along the way, until a satisfactory routine and series of subroutines are installed in the thought processes to automatically carry out the required task.

The Law of Delayed Effect

This is suggesting to the mind that a thought process and action will happen in the future at a specific time or event. We all have internal chronometers inside our heads that keep the time for us and alert us when a specific time has arrived.

If you programme yourself to get up at a specific time six mornings of the week, what time do you think you are likely to wake up on the seventh? Have you ever gone to bed and told yourself that you have to get up at a specific time and suddenly woken up a few minutes before the alarm went off?

Your conscious mind may not know what time it is but your unconscious mind counts the seconds, hours, days and months. Therefore you can suggest to yourself that something will happen in the future and it will. Do that while you are in a trance (post-hypnotic suggestion) and the suggestion will be even stronger. Repeat that suggestion each time you are in trance and the imprint on the mind becomes even stronger still.

> *I WILL SMILE EACH TIME I SEE MY BOSS*
> *I WILL REMEMBER TO READ EACH NIGHT*
> *I WILL DEEPLY RELAX EACH TIME I GO INTO A TRANCE*
> *I WILL FEEL VERY GOOD ABOUT BEING A NON-SMOKER EVERY DAY*
> *I WILL BE CONFIDENT WHEN I ADDRESS THE MEETING*

Be aware that you have a choice about what you put into your mind. Most people, however, are not aware of that and they go through their whole life performing many of the suggestions that other people, advertisers, and government propaganda put into their head.

Using the Dissociated Window

Many people can become disturbed about what has happened, is happening or will happen to them. Although they perceive themselves to be affected by what the outside world is doing to them (reactive thinking), they are in fact being panicked, upset, over-emotionalised and disturbed from the inside out. They have what is called a subjective perspective, which means their position considers everything through their own eyes. This, at times, does not give a person enough information to consider a situation rationally.

Disassociation Exercise 1 (Script)

I can sit and think of an unpleasant thing that happened to me recently ...feeling associated to that time...place...and experience...***BEING INSIDE MY OWN BODY...LOOKING OUT OF MY EYES...HEARING WHAT I HEARD...AND FEELING WHAT I FELT***...I can note how unpleasant it is and how out of control I believed I was...I can recognise the helplessness I was experiencing...***I CAN STEP OUTSIDE THAT EXPERIENCE***...watch myself from a distance...see how I am reacting to the situation... ***EXPERIENCING DETACHMENT FROM THE ME I AM OBSERVING*** ...analyse what that person is saying in their head...what voices are they hearing...***LISTEN TO THEIR THOUGHTS***...I can notice how their thoughts ...internal voices...and perceived subjectivity makes them feel...being aware they feel out of control...***I CAN ADVISE THEM FROM A DISTANCE HOW TO THINK***...***HAVE INTERNAL VOICES***...***AND SEE PICTURES DIFFERENTLY*** ...noticing how they change...seeing how they gain control and feel better...***I CAN STEP BACK INTO THE MORE CONTROLLED BODY AND MIND***...being aware how things look...sound...and feel differently...enjoying this feeling of control to choose how I act...***ALL THE WAY BACK INSIDE MYSELF MORE IN CONTROL***.

Disassociation Exercise 2

Find someone who you feel has annoyed you in the past. Before you approach them, *disassociate*, step outside the experience in your mind, reconstructing everything in your mind's eye, as if you were watching the whole thing on a television screen. See how much more you are in control of the situation, not experiencing the excess flooding of emotions. When you feel in control step back into your own body.

It gets easier to disassociate as you practise doing it whenever a past memory plagues you or you feel out of control. Never again let your unpleasant memories take control of you. Everything we go through in life is a learning experience and each time we go through those unpleasant memories we do not have to go through the whole emotional turmoil again. By disassociating you have learnt to look at the learning experience and not be a slave to the unpleasant feelings you once had. Practising disassociation, you can notice how much easier it is to remember the pleasant things when you want to and not have to re-experience the unpleasant ones.

Installing Personal Integrity

Everyone has personal integrity and for each of us it is composed of the maintaining of different sets of values. In one way no one person's set of values are more superior than anyone else's; however, there are commonly recognised sets of values that lead to a global view about what life principles allow a person to have integrity.

In Christian cultures, having integrity does, to some extent, mean that a person needs to adhere to laws based around the 10 commandments. In Jewish cultures, integrity is much more tied up with the cohesion of family maintenance and traditional values. In Muslim cultures, it is often tied up with a sense of honour. In India, integrity is very caste based and to stray out of your caste can be seen as losing your integrity. In China, integrity was, for a long time, connected with keeping the communist ideals.

Here we are mainly concerned with evaluating, strengthening and recognising your own integrity. This is the constant cohesion of the values you need to live your life in an active and rewarding way, which also adds to the lives of others.

Values
Choose the 10 most important values to you and write them down as they come to you. Then look at them after you have made the list and rearrange them in the order of importance that could best suit your life. Memorise the list and lock it away in a personal space like a diary or box of letters (see exercise on p158).

Remember, this is an exercise that you can go back to and do again at any time in your life because people, circumstances and lives change. *Flexibility* and *adaptability* are the most necessary qualities needed for any individual to survive throughout their life. Having a sense of integrity gives a person strong concepts of the borders between their own identity and the identities of others. Integrity helps a person believe in their own abilities and rights to have a place in society. A sense of your own integrity maintains the well being of the personality and physical health, giving a solid foundation for self-respect.

Integrity through Affirming Values (Script)
In each thing that I do I use my values to guide me...the self respect I create for myself can be founded on the values I believe in...***I CAN COMFORTABLY HAVE A SET OF WELL FORMED VALUES***...evolving as a human being I can examine my set of values...placing them in order of importance as I plan my life...***IN ORDER OF IMPORTANCE MY VALUES CAN HELP ME HAVE A SENSE OF INTEGRITY***...it's good to be aware of my own boundaries in relation to the world...sense where I finish and the world begins...***HAVING INTEGRITY HELPS GIVE ME MORE CONFIDENCE***...this all helps me to have the self-respect that guides me to my personal best...when I respect myself others are more likely to follow my example...***VALUES***...***INTEGRITY***...***AND SELF-RESPECT MAKE ME FEEL GOOD ABOUT MYSELF***.

Owning Your Natural Potential
As you are now aware I am totally convinced of your potential to be a genius as in my eyes everyone is a genius simply because they are human. What I strongly believe is that because of the way societies are structured you have been brainwashed into believing that you are not highly intelligent nor have endless amounts of natural resources.

I HAVE ALL THE ABILITIES I NEED TO LIVE MY LIFE WITH EXCELLENCE

I met a 60-year-old black American woman down in New Orleans who had been a street walker until she was 40. When I met her she was working as a professor of English at a university. She told me how she grew up in poverty and had no expectations about her future until one day she decided she was getting too old for the life she had been leading and needed to do something else. Once her values and belief systems about her abilities changed, her self-respect rocketed and she found a sense of integrity that no one had told her was possible for a black woman from the swamps in the 1960s.

What is important about her story is that she found belief in herself. If she had found belief in her abilities and still decided to remain a street walker that would also have been OK. None of us have any right to judge her but what we can do is celebrate her acquisition of choice.

Reading this work you know I do not know about your personal circumstances but you are becoming aware that I believe you can do almost anything you set your mind to do. What I want you to remember is that this is my fourth book and I did not have a fancy education, grew up in poverty and thought that happy families was simply a card game. In fact between the ages of 11 and 15 I did not have an education at all because I had been placed in a state home. Add to this the fact that I am dyslexic, and you might begin to understand the kind of strong belief I have had to create in myself to become a well respected therapist and writer whose books sell all over the world.

As you continue to learn to build your positive values, integrity, self-respect and esteem, and belief in yourself, attitudes and potential abilities change. I have a personal motto which you can install as an unshakeable belief:

WHATEVER IT TAKES, I HAVE IT

Helplessness is not on my menu because I believe that there is always a way to make something happen and if I do not have the knowledge I go out and find someone who has that knowledge. If they know how to do whatever I want to happen, either they can do it for me, help me to do it or help me learn how to do it. The most important thing is that whatever it is gets done.

Of course, being realistic about the goals that you set yourself is vital. If you have one leg then you are unlikely to win the Tour de France bicycle race. At 15 years of age you are unlikely to be voted the president or prime minister. Evaluate the possibilities sensibly and then time your chances of completing your goal by 10 and 10 again, remembering I believe in you and you can believe in yourself. Now do the exercise on p163.

A few years ago my mother, at the age of 69, was involved in a head-on car crash which broke her ankles, legs, ribs, arms, punctured her lungs and very nearly killed her. When I saw her in the hospital she was black, blue and yellow from tip to toe. It took the fireman hours to cut her out of the wreckage of the car and when she got to the hospital it was a touch and go situation. After several painful operations over six years she now walks, talks and is still

41

spending the winter in Portugal or North Africa.

Her recovery has been quite remarkable and when I asked how she had done it she told me that she had made up her mind that illness was not an option. She had installed the right mindset at the very beginning that she was going to recover and carry on with her life. She had the right kind of mindset that would give her the strength and determination to get where she wanted to go.

People are encouraged in society to give up too easily and settle for second best in their lives. They are constantly teased by the riches and luxury they see on television that they think will never be available for them, which deems them second-class citizens. They are pacified by governments to do the lottery and depend on having a one in a zillion chance of having the kind of consumerist irrelevance that they think they should have. Most people never learn to tap into their own natural brilliance in their lives until they hit a crisis.

At 42 Victor had to leave the army because his wife had been killed. He was now the only parent for his four small children under five who he had not seen very much because he had spent a lot of time away on active duty. Although he could strip a rifle and put it back together blindfolded, run a marathon, and drive endless different kinds of tanks he did not know how to change a nappy. Their home had been next to an army base many miles away from any of their immediate relatives so for all intents and purposes he was on his own.

Within five years he had set up a business from home on the internet, selling children's toys all over the world with the help of his children who became involved as testers, market researchers, promoters and distributors of those toys. At home they called themselves the toy army. He had adapted his need to make a living to fit the fact that he was a housebound ex-military single parent with four children to raise.

I AM THE GREATEST ASSET I HAVE

We all have individual characteristics that make us different and special, so learn to utilise those very positive traits in you that you have never considered using before. Be persistent in following your dreams, whatever they are, and do not let other people's negative attitudes contaminate your positive beliefs in yourself.

I often have to deal with academics and I can tell you that some of them become so superior minded, thinking that they are more intelligent than other people. It always makes me laugh because some of the best pieces of advice I have had in my life have come from the very simplest of souls who can see clearly because they are not bogged down with the trappings of dogma.

I am going to tell you about my Great Aunt Hilda and Great Uncle Joe. Great Aunt Hilda had both breasts off at 38 due to breast cancer and the doctors told her to go home and put her affairs in order as she had only six weeks to live. However, she had two small children whom she was determined not to leave alone after the dreadful economic depression of the 1930s. She told the doctors she absolutely refused to follow their instructions, went home and carried on as a swimming instuctress. Just the other month Great Aunt Hilda was 100 years old. Where do you think the doctors are?

When I was small I used to ask Great Uncle Joe how old he was and he would reply: "More than 80 and not yet the 100 I am going to be when I get my telegram from the Queen". He had worked all his life down the coal mine and told me that it was a very hard existence and after he had retired he had made up his mind to get as much free coal on his pension as he could because he reckoned he had earned it. When he died at 102 people had to wait around until they settled the matter of who was going to take his library book back, and when a promise had been made he then decided to die.

Owning Your Natural Potential (Script)

I can own the quest of continually exploring my natural potential...expecting of myself more than I have ever done before...**MY LIFE CAN BE A PROCESS OF CONTINUAL GROWTH AND OWNING MY NATURAL POTENTIAL**...time to recognise that I have a genius within me...I have amazing amounts of untapped resources...**I CAN RECOGNISE THE GENIUS WITHIN**...as I examine my beliefs about myself I can reassess...taking time to install new more positive beliefs...**I CAN BELIEVE IN MYSELF**...whatever I want to do I can find a way to make it happen...need can be the source of invention...**EACH DAY I CAN REINVENT MYSELF**...life is a quest of learning to control my mind...body...and spirit...it can be a challenge I enjoy being part of...**I WILL VIEW LIFE AS AN OPPORTUNITY TO EXCEL**...it is possible to positively construct my thoughts...building upon all the successes I have had...**I AM USING LANGUAGE AS A POSITIVE TOOL NOW!**...I have whatever it takes to be the person I want to be...it can be seen that persistence pays off...**I CAN APPLY MYSELF REPETITIOUSLY TO HELP ACHIEVE MY GOALS**...there are good suggestions that I can make to myself daily...being aware of the progress I make...**I AM MY GREATEST ASSET AND I CAN TREASURE MYSELF**...it is good to be in control of life...positively constructing a sense of excellence...**I EMBRACE MY GOALS**...**HOPES**...**AND DREAMS** ...**OWNING THEM AND MAKING THEM REAL**...whatever I need to do I can find a way...helping myself...others...and accepting kindness...**EACH DAY BEFORE I AWAKE I CAN SEE THE SUN RISE INSIDE MY HEAD**.

Summary

■ Own your natural potential, learn to recognise your ability to change and take control of your life.

■ Understanding the difference between the active and reactive modes of behaviour and how to move into the positive active state.

■ Doing the *now* exercise to bring yourself back into the present experience of living and realising that you are successful already by simply being alive.

■ Realising the power and effectiveness of self-suggestion that can change your behaviour and thinking about yourself and life.

■ Recognising that the beliefs you have permit, deny, promote or restrict behaviour. Changing those beliefs and installing new ones to empower you to become whatever you want to be.

■ Structuring positive affirmations to programme yourself to act out tasks in the present and future.

■ Applying discipline and repetition to your mind and actions to make things happen as a matter of habit as well as exception.

■ Using disassociation in your mind to give you a better perspective of what is happening to you and how you can take information from the new viewpoint and apply it constructively to your life.

■ Working out your values and prioritising them to give you integrity, beliefs and attitudes.

■ Owning your natural brilliance by realising you are your greatest asset you will ever encounter.

■ Do the exercises on p159 and p162.

Frequently Asked Questions

Q. Suppose I have not always been such a nice person and my values used to be different?

A. We are all growing, learning, evolving to become the person we would like to be and would like others to think we are. It is natural to always be on a learning curve because it is when you think you are perfect that you are in trouble.

Q. If I practise disassociation, am I likely to get too spaced out?

A. There are some people who have psychological conditions that cause them to be permanently spaced out – they have little contact with reality, but this does not happen to the average person. Learning to move into an imaginary disassociated position where you view your life objectively is not only healthy but a sign of maturity. Because you are able to tell the difference between an associated and disassociated state and how to get from one to the other, this gives you power over your life. Associate again back into your body after each trance during your everyday waking life.

Q. As I get good at going into a trance can I try doing it to someone else?

A. The answer is definitely not, unless you are a trained hypnotist and that takes a great deal of study, far beyond the capacity of this book. Healthcare professionals are also insured, should anything go wrong as well as being trained to a very high standard. It would not be fair to the other person unless you are a trained hypnotist.

Q. Do I need to practise self-hypnosis so regularly?
A. What you put into your life will determine what you get out and the quality of those results, as that is the basis of the law of cause and effect. Practising self-hypnosis every day will give you an enormous number of benefits as have been mentioned, and will empower you to have control over your life. If you are good to yourself and accept your amazing ability to do so many things with hypnosis every day, think how wonderful you will feel.

Further Reading

BUZAN, TONY, **USE YOUR HEAD**, BBC BOOKS, LONDON, 1974.

BUZAN, TONY, **THE MINDMAP BOOK**, BBC BOOKS, LONDON, 1993.

DEPORTER, BOBBI & HERNACKI, MIKE, **QUANTUM LEARNING: UNLEASH THE GENIUS WITHIN YOU**, PIATKUS PUBLISHERS, LONDON, 1993.

DRYDEN, GORDON & VOS, JEANNETTE, **THE LEARNING REVOLUTION**, ACCELERATED LEARNING SYSTEMS, BUCKS, UK, 1994.

HALLBOM, TIM & SMITH, SUZI, **BELIEFS: PATHWAYS TO HEALTH & WELL BEING**, METAMORPHOUS PRESS, OR, USA, 1990.

HUTCHISON, MICHAEL, **MEGA BRAIN**, BALLANTINE BOOKS, NEW YORK, 1986.

HUTCHISON, MICHAEL, **MEGA BRAIN POWER: TRANSFORM YOUR LIFE WITH MIND MACHINES AND BRAIN NUTRIENTS**, HYPERION, NEW YORK, 1994.

JENSEN, ERIC, **THE LEARNING BRAIN**, TURNING POINT PUBLISHING, SAN DIEGO, USA, 1995.

JOUDRY, PATRICIA, **SOUND THERAPY FOR THE WALKMAN**, STEELE & STEELE, DALMENY, CANADA, 1984.

O'BRIEN, DOMINIC, **HOW TO DEVELOP A PERFECT MEMORY**, HEADLINE BOOK PUBLISHING, LONDON, 1993.

SARTRE, JEAN-PAUL, **EXISTENTIALISM AND HUMANISM**, METHUEN &

CO, LONDON, 1948.

SCHEELE, PAUL R, **THE PHOTOREADING WHOLE MIND SYSTEM**, LEARN-ING STRATEGIES CORPORATION, MINNESOTA, USA, 1993.

SCHEELE, PAUL R, **NATURAL BRILLIANCE: MOVE FROM FEELING STUCK TO ACHIEVING SUCCESS**, LEARNING STRATEGIES CORPORATION, MINNESOTA, USA, 1997.

WENGER, WIN, PhD & POE, RICHARD, **THE EINSTEIN FACTOR**, PRIMA PUBLISHING, CA, USA, 1995.

Chapter Four

Hypnotic Re-Education of Breathing

"Breath is life"
Yogi Ramacharaka

From our very first breath we spend the whole of our lives inhaling oxygen and exhaling carbon dioxide and water, which are some of the waste products of the body. Our lungs are a complex structure of branches, starting with the trachea, sub-dividing into the bronchi, then the bronchioles and finally the alveolar ducts and sacs. The intricate tree-like structures of the surface of the lungs produce the square surface area of a tennis court where the exchange of gases takes place in what is called the respiratory zone. During our lifetime we take many millions of breaths...**OXYGEN IS THE BREATH OF LIFE**...and without it there is no life.

This exchange of gases in the lungs is called **EXTERNAL RESPIRATION** and provides the red blood cells in the blood system with renewed resources of oxygen to transport to the different parts of the body. There it fires with fuel like glucose to produce energy and also has the very important role of cleansing the body because oxygen is a natural neutraliser of toxins. The exchange of oxygen for carbon dioxide and water in the cells is called **INTERNAL RESPIRATION**.

Having two lungs in humans enables us to increase or decrease our oxygen intake according to the particular needs of the moment. It also gives us a back-up system should one lung fail, deflate or suffer from disease. The right lung is larger than the left because there needs to be room on the left hand side of the body to accommodate the heart. During exercise the requirements of oxygen needed to fuel the muscle tissue is increased dramatically, and during sedentary moments our need for oxygen is decreased. Each organ also regulates its own need for oxygen and blood through what is called **METABOLIC AUTOREGULATION**.

The brain always needs at least 15 per cent of the oxygen we use and even if our oxygen levels drop, the brain does not reduce its requirements for that amount. The brain cells are very delicate and need to operate at a constant level so that no damage occurs. You might think of the brain and spinal cord (central nervous system) as a very fine mainframe computer that needs to be protected from any changes in environment, atmosphere, elements or interruption of power supply.

We can generally hold our breaths for three minutes at the most but very experienced yogis or escapologists have been known to hold their breath for more than 13 minutes and reduce their breathing dramatically for hours, even days.

When oxygen has been cut off to the brain it causes hypoxia (starvation of oxygen) and can result in severe and permanent brain damage. If a child is born with the umbilical cord wrapped around its neck there can be damage to the foetus's brain during the birth process.

Reduction of oxygen to the lungs due to obstruction of the respiratory passages causes illness and eventually death. Poor quality air with low levels of oxygen or higher levels of toxins can also cause damage to the body, immune system and cognitive (thinking) process over a longer period of time.

If oxygen supply to any tissue is cut off, the tissue will die. One of the most common examples of this is coronary heart disease (CHD) where the blood vessels that supply the heart are blocked by lipids (fats), cellular debris and calcium salts. The blocked blood vessel condition is called arteriosclerosis and part of the heart muscle then dies (myocardial ischaemia) due to narrowing in the vessels and lack of nutrients and oxygen. Afterwards when the person exercises or exerts themselves they suffer from pains of the heart (angina). In extreme cases this causes so much tissue death in the heart muscle that the person has a heart attack.

Similar situations in the brain can occur when blockages of the blood vessels in the head happen and a person has a stroke. The brain is starved of nutrients and oxygen with the effect causing part of the brain tissue to die.

Through empirical studies we can see that these blockages are due to poor diet, hypertension (when the blood vessels are insufficiently elastic), lack of exercise, and most of all smoking, which causes massive damage to the respiratory, blood and immune systems. However, such blockages can also occur due to circulatory malfunction, damage, deformation, inherited genetic body types and over clotting of the blood (deep vein thrombosis).

So...**OXYGEN IS THE BREATH OF LIFE**...and we can live very well with sufficient supplies of it but we cannot be well if we are deprived of it in any way. There are many hundreds of different kinds of breathing patterns. Some belong to different medical models and others belong to philosophical and/or physical disciplines like yoga, meditation, re-birthing, and different kinds of athletics.

We shall be looking at breathing for changing your body and mind later in this chapter.

A few years ago I met a man who had been travelling the world studying different forms of meditation with many of the great teachers. I was fascinated talking to him and hearing about what seemed to be his endless knowledge of breath. Eventually, after telling me about all his teachers and the places he had studied, he apologised for having learnt only 700 ways of breathing.

Although I have talked about major lack of oxygen so far, there is also what is called *chronic oxygen deprivation* when a person may have shallow and poor breathing patterns. They inhale low levels of air, causing long-term lack of oxygen. That in turn affects the metabolism of the body and also helps create sluggishness, poor brain function, depression, constipation, irritable bowel syndrome (IBS) and physical and mental blockages that occur due to the non-completion of the *sedation/excitation* cycle of life. Many chronically ill people have poor breathing patterns, insufficient supplies of oxygen and they may also have inhibited and repressed behaviour patterns.

The learning of this shallow breathing pattern can be due to trauma, poor behaviour training or adjustment to earlier difficult situations in their lives. They may come from a family where parents or others have had shallow breathing patterns and they have learnt to copy that style.

The **SHALLOW BREATHER** represses their bodily functions to be minimal, appearing as if they are not really there. Perhaps they may have grown up in an atmosphere where expressing yourself was not encouraged so they were taught to be very quiet and not use their body in a naturally variant way. They may also have been subject to trauma of differing kinds and experienced intimidation from adults, abuse and bullying from siblings, or sensed danger about being out in the world.

Such people often avoid confrontation of any kind and remain vegetative and withdrawn. They have low confidence, poor eye contact and can become resentful of and defensive towards people who try to engage their interest and initiate a provocative interaction with them.

They have learned to keep still and frozen like a fox in the headlights of a car. They are inhibitionists and suppressers, not only of their social behaviour, but also of their bodily functions too. Shallow breathers can also suffer from asthma, stomach problems, fatigue and poor blood circulation.

Strong or particular colours, sounds, touches, smells or tastes can cause them to be evasive or retreat. These can trigger unconscious memories of the original incidents or programming that led up to them becoming shallow breathers. Sex can often seem very frightening for them as they do not perceive themselves as being in control of their lives and feel vulnerable.

Because the body is not getting sufficient quantities of oxygen they do not break through the act-react cycle of behaviour. They tend to be reactive to things rather than acting on their own cognisance and initiating ways forward for themselves. Inhibitionists can make very good hypnotic subjects and tend to daydream a lot of their time. The day dreaming can become morbid and focused on worst case scenarios as they often have little belief in their own abilities. When shallow breathers become millionaires or successful it is not because they want to but because they are afraid not to be.

OVER BREATHERS suffer from a condition called *hyperventilation syndrome* which means they are breathing too fast and often. They are generally in a state of high anxiety, panic and alarm. Their breath intake is concentrated in the upper respiratory area of the nose and upper head which means they are very prone to colds, flu, sinus, ear, nose and throat infections, flem, tension, high levels of stress, headaches, migraines, and they often suffer from shortness of breath when they panic.

Sometimes over breathers also have periods when they breathe quickly and then they will stop breathing all of a sudden. At this time they believe that they cannot get their breath but it is their brain telling them to slow down their breathing and breathe more deeply.

Over breathers concentrate the focus of their breath in their upper respiratory tract and in the centre of the face, and they do not breath deeply. The intercostal muscles, between the ribs, do not fully expand or contract to allow sufficient amounts of air into the lungs to replenish the body's oxygen levels. Also the diaphragm muscle beneath the lungs does not completely expand in order to lower the air pressure, allowing new and fresh air to rush into the lungs.

Because when we breathe normally only part of the air in the lungs is exchanged, deep breathing is needed to fully re-oxygenate our blood. Since hyperventilation occurs in the upper respiratory tract and upper chest the deeper regions of the lungs do not exchange their gases.

The part of the brain that controls respiration detects this low level of oxygen and gives orders to the lungs to extract more oxygen from the air and exhale more carbon dioxide. However, since the over breather does not deep breathe, all that happens is that they continue to breathe faster and faster in the upper respiratory tract and upper chest.

During the flight or fight response, when we either have to face danger or run away from it, our respiration needs to increase dramatically in order to give the skeletal muscles enough oxygen and energy to face the perceived physical or psychological danger or run from it. The over breather, however, because they are breathing so fast, unconsciously believes they are in the constant state of alarm that exists within the flight or fight response. It is a feedback loop which has become so automatic that they are unaware of what is happening at a conscious level.

When shallow breathing and over breathing patterns are chronic dysfunctions they are unnaturally depriving the body of good levels of oxygen sufficient for a person to be in prime physical and psychological health. Thinking processes become stuck, slow, sluggish or so panicked that the person is unable to process information in a way that can seem clear and succinct.

In disorders like manic depression a person is depressed and hyperactive, alternately moving from shallow to over breathing. Such people believe that their physical and mental symptoms are totally out of their control. These switches can happen over several days or even in the space of a few minutes. Retraining the person to have control over their breathing as well as their thinking patterns can do much more than the over prescription of drugs, without the terrible side effects caused by many medications.

Even though there are some disorders and diseases that cannot be rectified by adjusting and re-educating a person's breathing patterns, for the majority of people, hypnotic re-education of breath can change their lives both mentally and physically to a monumental extent. For thousands of years yogis and hypnotists have been using breathing to alter people's physical, mental and spiritual states and improve their lives...***GOOD RESPIRATION PROMOTES GOOD PHYSICAL AND MENTAL HEALTH***.

Oxygen binds with a pigment present in red blood cells called haemoglobin to form oxyhaemoglobin. If insufficient or poor external respiration is taking place then the blood does not carry enough oxyhaemoglobin to re-oxygenate the tissues and carry away the waste products. Poor quality air with low oxygen content can cause people to become ill and depressed. Since more than two thirds of the world's population now live in cities, where air quality is poor, people are generally suffering from oxygen starvation but are unaware of what is happening to them.

One of the most ironic socio-economic observations we can make is that some of the most expensive areas of London, such as Mayfair and Marylebone are among the most polluted. So money and up-market real-estate does not necessarily mean cleaner air.

What also happens in cities is that the high carbon dioxide and carbon monoxide content in the air prevents the uptake of oxygen in the bloodstream and the release of oxygen from the blood into the tissue that needs re-oxygenating. Furthermore the high levels of exhaust fumes and pollutants in the inner city atmosphere inhibit people's red blood cells, reducing even more their ability to re-oxygenate the body.

So by...***RELEARNING THE WAY YOU BREATHE***...*you* can change the effectiveness of how you function as a human being. What I would like you to clearly understand is that you can very easily change the way you breathe by physical and mental reprogramming exercises. This is also not dependent on age as older people can just as easily reprogramme their breathing as anyone else.

When I was studying singing in my late teens with an Italian professor of voice, the first three months were spent just on breathing, without singing a single note, learning to support the voice. Gymnasts, dancers and athletes use different kinds of breathing patterns to promote physical momentum and control their posture. A few years ago I spent a day with a famous yoga teacher who talked to me about the different kinds of breathing he used to help practitioners relax, focus on the breath to open up their bodies, cleanse their systems, and change their mental states.

Hypnotists use changes in breathing to induce trance and different mental states during hypnosis which can release blocked emotions, generate new physical states and evolve new thought patterns.

One of the things that doctors and therapists note when they take detailed case histories from their patients/clients is that many people who later in life present with anxiety and depression were asthma sufferers when they were younger. Although some people have respiratory disorders the vast majority of asthma sufferers are, in fact, suffering from psychosomatic dysfunctional breathing patterns. Once they have been taught how to re-educate their breathing many of their problems go away and they no longer need medication or ventilators.

The modern home is a veritable trap for the kind of conditions that promote respiratory irritants. Carpets harbour an army of bugs and housemites and no matter what kind of vacuum cleaner you have the more hard surfaces you have in your home the less provocative the environment is to bad breathing conditions. The modern western home also has poor ventilation and pockets of stale air lurking in the corners. Double glazing adds to the stagnant air by trapping it when ventilation and new air from the outside is needed. In large buildings the recycling of the same poor quality air that often contains other people's germs is referred to as *sick building syndrome.*

Blowback from drains, sewage and gas can cause noxious effects without a person being consciously aware of the effects that the environment may be having on health or behaviour. Fresh air is one of the great contributors to health and well being because it has a higher oxygen content.

Poor breathers need to increase their physical activity to exercise aerobically three times a week for at least 20-30 minutes a time. They also need to do stretching exercises in order to move the oxygen around the body and promote stretching in the abdomen and rib cage muscles. If this is done in the gym then it does need to be under the guidance of an instructor and they may need to start the programme gently at first and slowly increase. Not only does this increase oxygen intake during those times of exercise but it also breaks the constancy of old shallow breathing patterns.

What is equally important is that it agitates the digestive system so that food is naturally moved along the gut and unnatural constipation of food does not take place. Our bodies are designed to go out and find food, and becoming couch potatoes means that we are not getting the kind of exercise that promotes good breathing.

Each morning you can re-educate your breathing by standing outside the front door in the fresh air. Take long, slow, deep breaths in through the nose and exhale through the mouth, counting very slowly to 20 for each breath cycle. On the in breath slowly stretch your arms up sideways above your head and on the out breath slowly allow them to reverse gently by your sides. As you do this close your eyes and visualise beautiful oxygen coming into your lungs, helping your body to re-oxygenate your blood, tissues, and brain. On the out breath...let all your unnecessary tension and troubles go off...

TROUBLES OUT ON THE OUT BREATH INTO THE DISTANCE
...FAR...FAR...AWAY

Memorise the following script inside your head in your own voice for good breathing and think it to yourself as you do this exercise, seeing yourself inside your own mind:

REMEMBER BREATHE IN AS YOUR ARMS COME UP TO THE COUNT OF 20...AND OUT AS THEY SLOWLY DESCEND BY YOUR SIDE

Breath of Life (Script)

Through my nose I can breathe in beautiful oxygen...filling my body naturally with energy...*I TAKE IN THE BREATH OF LIFE*...out of my mouth flows any unnecessary tension...stress can leave me...*MY TROUBLES FLOAT AWAY*...I slowly breathe in through my nose as my arms raise...enjoying control over my good body...*PURE OXYGEN CLEANSING EVERY PART OF ME*...through my mouth leave the wastes from my body...I respect and say goodbye to them...*I AM LEFT FEELING WHOLE*...through my nose I take in the breath of life...nature knows how to heal me...*I BECOME THE OXYGEN I BREATHE*...through my mouth I thank the breath that leaves me...I am centred and at one with myself...*CLEANSED...PURE...AND IN LOVE WITH MY OWN BODY*. (Learn and repeat over to yourself without a formal induction each morning as you do the breathing exercises).

In China many people do martial arts every morning and while they are doing the exercises they are also visualising and thinking about the relationship of their bodies to the flow of energy. In the West we are so caught up with coping with modern life that we often forget the real point of our labours. Is it time for you to fall in love with your body once more?

DO YOU WORK TO EAT OR EAT TO WORK?

Despite inheriting a lot of our body types it is possible to overcome much of the genetic expression and take control over our health. You often see young men on television who were puny, skinny, thin and bullied when they were young. Several years later, however, after they have taken up body building and exercised they have become beautiful specimens of manhood who win body building contests and find themselves surrounded by potential suitors.

Overweight sedentary people who were bullied at school can also lose a great deal of weight when they grow up and turn into swans, just like the ugly duckling, who one day realised that it was not really a duckling after all.

Two years ago I had an 85-year-old-woman come to see me after having lost her confidence due to being in hospital for six weeks with pneumonia. After a few sessions I co-ordinated with her doctor and a health club to enable her to take up weight lifting for a reduced fee. Now she has no trace of her previous illness, tells me she is fitter than she has been for 30 years, enjoys her morning journeys to the gym and has made a whole new set of friends, some of whom are a quarter of her age. Her lungs are working just fine.

Medication is not always the best way to go because more than half of the medications that you buy at your chemist today have side effects that doctors never even bother to tell you about. People get into the habit of becoming over dependent on medications and less in tune with the natural resources their body has to offer them. Never refuse medication when you are in a life or death situation but think carefully the next time you are offered a quick fix out of a bottle and its long-term effects.

Another client of mine came to see me after 25 years of various forms of sleeping pills and antidepressants. His doctor was very against him coming to see a hypnotherapist, telling the client that he did not think it was proper medicine. He had not been able to work for 10 years because he believed he was depressed, his wife believed he was depressed, and his whole family also knew how to do that belief. They were comfortable with the belief that their father was depressed and reluctant to give it up.

Part of my prescription for him was that he go and learn to breathe with a Chinese teacher in the East End of London right next to where he lived. I did not tell him that he had to learn Tai-Chi from the Master, only that he was to go to him and ask him for a five-year course on breathing, including daily instruction. After six months he was not taking any pills, no longer believed he was depressed, practised Tai-Chi twice a day in the park and did the accounts for the Chinese teacher I had sent him to see.

I am now going to teach you eight breathing positions that I teach to my clients and as you learn them I want you to move the focus of your breathing physically and in your mind. Experience the vibrations in your body, bones and muscles as the different parts of you vibrate when those areas become a point of focus.

1. Chest Breathing This is chest breathing just like a sergeant major does on parade in the army. The chest is the main point of focus as it moves up and down and in and out as you breathe in and exhale. You are leading with your chest.

2. Throat Breathing Be aware of the breath moving in and out of your open throat as you hear the air gasping in the windpipe. For this to happen both your mouth and nasal passages are open and clear as well as your throat.

3. Mouth Breathing Open your mouth wide and feel the air drying your lips, tongue and inner cheeks as you labour only in the mouth region as you breathe in and out.

4. Central Nasal Breathing This takes place in the middle parts of the face through the nose. It is a very sniffy sort of sound as if someone is trying to speak when they have a cold. People who suffer a lot from nasal infections habitually breathe focused in this region.

5. Zygomatic Nasal Breathing This is a wider kind of nasal breathing that happens when people are panicking and the cheekbones vibrate fiercely. The cheek muscles are also tight over the cheekbones. Over breathers and people with high anxiety and stress levels focus their breath here. Singers feel similar vibrations on their cheekbones when they sing higher notes, particularly in opera. It is possible to be doing either kind of nasal breathing or changing from one to the other.

6. Head Breathing In times of absolute panic when a person is in the highest state of alarm (brain patterns in High Beta wave activity) their breathing can be focused on the two parietal bones at the side of the head and the frontal bone at the forehead, making them experience dizziness, paranoia, and confusion.

7. Stomach Breathing With your mouth open, lead with your stomach muscles. Place your hand on your stomach, feeling and watching it going in and out but do not breathe with any other part of you. Feel the stomach muscles working.

8. Peach Breathing This is the breathing of deep trance and meditation when everything has slowed down. Close your eyes and imagine that there are two small inflatable sacks about the size of peaches in the small of your back just where your kidneys reside. They are like little bellows because each time you breathe in they fill with air and when you breathe out they deflate.

These peach-sized bellows are, however, the only place you breathe with your mouth open and your airways clear. Make them the colour of great relaxation in your mind and see the air that comes in as that relaxing colour. All the cares you have in the world can float out off on your out breath. Peach breathing happens very slowly and the bellows are the only parts of your body that are moving.

In order to retrain your breathing it is necessary to practise it daily, consciously at first for 10 minutes at a time. In time this will then become an automatic pattern that you can utilise when you get into a situation that used to be unnecessarily stressful to you, but now you move into calm peach breathing. Let your body have breathing exercise as well as all the other kinds of maintenance. The new breathing patterns will start as a conscious behaviour, then become an unconscious automatic reaction.

Shallow and hyperventilation breathers are always upper head, mouth, throat and upper chest breathers. In moments of stress they move into the breathing patterns associated with alarm and panic or frozen postures. Unfortunately they often do not realise when the states of alarm are over so they continue to have the breathing patterns of someone who is not deep breathing. They can feel tired, run down, stressed, low in energy, confused, afraid and lacking in confidence. They can have erratic and unsatisfactory sleeping patterns or feel up one minute and down the next.

Because over breathers are continually swallowing they can also have very bad digestive problems including constant burping, bloating, indigestion, flatulence and heartburn. A vicious cycle sets in as breathing gets faster and focused higher in the body yet the person never gets enough oxygen in the lungs because of the low volumes consumed and the speed with which the air leaves the lungs.

During hyperventilation the brain is in High Beta wave activity a great deal of the time and the person remains in the flight or fight response, perceiving themselves to be in danger, at an unconscious level, when that may not be so. This constant state of alarm puts stresses on their body and particularly the immune system.

Practising, Locating, Having Control Over, and Utilising Peach Breathing to Retrain Your Breathing Patterns
You can make a recording on a tape of the following exercises in your own voice or a hypnotist or therapist can do it for you if you find their voice calming. Eventually, however, after one week you can make the recording yourself, listen to it each day and memorise every step of the exercise.

Play the tape on a personal stereo as you stand in front of a large mirror, legs apart the width of your hips, arms resting loosely by your sides, knees slightly bent, shoulders relaxed, mouth open, and watching your body. Eventually after many practices dispense with the mirror and sense each movement in your body as you learn to shift the focus of your breathing. Finally dispense with the recording and take the exercise as your own. Learn the script by heart so you can utilise peach breathing whenever you need to.

Learning to Move to Peach Breathing (Script)
My body can be aware of my breathing...what is normally unconscious can be conscious...***BEING AWARE OF MY CHEST RISING AND FALLING***...no other part of my body is in focus...breathing happens in my chest...***BIG BREATHS ALL THE WAY IN AND ALL THE WAY OUT***...my throat can open all the way up...like a hollow cavity it is a vessel for travelling air...***I SENSE AIR PASSING DOWN MY THROAT AND AIR PASSING UP AGAIN***...no other part of my body moves...inside my throat the air moves freely...***BIG BREATHS ALL THE WAY IN AND ALL THE AIR OUT***...I become aware of the air in my mouth...only breathing through my mouth...***FEELING THE SECRETIONS IN MY MOUTH DRY***...it's good to have my mouth's airways

clear...my breathing is faster than before...***BIG BREATHS ALL THE WAY IN AND ALL THE AIR OUT***...breath focuses inside the centre of my nose ...breathing a little faster with each breath being shorter...***I AM AWARE OF THE AIR AND NASAL MUCUS***...faster and shorter and faster and shorter...I want to lean my body forwards...***THESE ARE SHORTER FASTER BREATHS AND SHORTER FASTER BREATHS***...my nasal breaths spread across my cheekbones and out into space...I am a wider upper nose breather...***I CAN FEEL MY CHEEKBONES VIBRATE***...the muscles of my face tense up...breathing faster and getting dizzy...***I AM AWARE OF BREATHING NASAL AND WIDE***...the upper sides of my head now vibrate...as the skull bones vibrate fast and rapid...***I RECOGNISE THE FEELING OF PANIC***...controlling my lack of control...I get dizzy and light headed...***I AM BREATHING FAST AND IN THE UPPER HEAD***...slowly I bring the breathing down back to the chest...there is no rush no hurry ...***THROUGH EACH STAGE MY BREATHING GETS SLOWER***...passing each breathing point...I can see my chest rising and falling...***BIG BREATHS ALL THE WAY IN AND ALL THE AIR OUT***...in my mind I see my incoming breath is calm...it has the colour of calm...***EACH BREATH I BREATHE IN IS THE COLOUR OF CALM***...my stomach breathes for me...no other part of my body moves...***ALL MY CARES FLOAT OFF ON THE OUT BREATH***...my breath is my friend...I breathe in the oxygen of life...***I BREATHE OUT THE WASTE FROM MY BODY AND THANK IT***...my peach breathing takes over ...no other part of my body moves...***I AM MY PEACH BREATHING***...each slow breath fills the peaches with calm...I am in a deep state of relaxation ...***MY INNER VOICE SAYS CALM...PEACE...PEACHES***...there's no rush and there's no hurry...I have the time I need to rest my body...***I AM MY CALM SLOW BREATH***...my breath and I are together in harmony...I see...hear ...and feel it...***I AM THE OXYGEN OF LIFE*** (Rest in trance for a few minutes leaving the tape running, recording silence during this time)...I can slowly reorientate myself to wakefulness...***REMEMBERING PEACH BREATHING WHENEVER I NEED...WANT...OR DESIRE***.

Butterflies with Oxygen

During trance you can use visualised images to re-oxygenate your blood unconsciously. See in your mind the wonderful spreading of an army of bright red butterflies, each one of them carrying a bucket of oxygen which they are going to give to every cell in your body. Let them slowly spread up from the bottom of your feet to the top of your head. Do not rush the image but take your time, allowing your body to feel lighter and lighter.

When you perceive that every cell in your body has been topped up with **REFRESHING OXYGEN** you will note that your breathing becomes deeper during the visualisation. Now extend the oxygen in your mind to about two feet away from your body so that you also bathe in its healing effects. Finally keep that image with you in some part of your mind for the rest of the trance and throughout the day.

Go out into the world and study breathing by buying all the books you can find on it, using and making self-hypnosis tapes for yourself and/or joining a yoga class. Enjoy, explore and learn breathing.

Summary

■ Being aware of the breath of life and how important oxygen is to your external and internal respiration, affecting the metabolic autoregulation of every single organ in your body.

■ Identifying the difference between shallow, over, upper respiratory tract and deep breathing.

■ Exercising to relearn the way you breathe at a conscious and then an unconscious level so that you breathe well automatically.

■ Locating the eight breathing positions and practising how to get from one to the other, utilising peach breathing for calmness and control.

■ Using the butterflies imagery in trance to take oxygen to each and every part of your body as it cleanses, heals and renews your tissues.

Frequently Asked Questions

Q. I was always a very sickly child and still suffer from asthma. Am I OK to do deep breathing exercises?

A. Without a doubt it is probably one of the best things you will ever do to promote health. It is commonly accepted now that free radicals, which are parts of leftover molecules in the blood, cause ageing, damage and illness. Oxygen helps eradicate those free radicals and promotes better health. Install the deep breathing routine in your morning every day, filling your lungs with the cheapest natural cure you will ever find…OXYGEN IS THE BREATH OF LIFE.

It does not matter what kind of food you eat or medication you take – if you have poor breathing patterns, they severely limit your life and what you are able to do physically and mentally.

Q. I am pregnant and have had three previous miscarriages. Is it safe for me to do the deep breathing?

A. If you are prone to miscarrying then you should not be moving around a great deal during pregnancy because you do not want your body to receive shocks or be exposed to any unnecessary stress. Do a milder version of the morning exercise but do a huge amount of self-hypnosis for calm, health and well being. It is essential that you attend your ante-natal clinic and talk about your situation with the nurse and the obstetrician. Talk to your baby in trance as it will respond to your communications and as you make friends with it you will give birth to a much calmer baby that will sleep better and have deeper breathing patterns.

Q. I don't think I would like doing the different breathing exercise because I would be afraid if I did the head breathing one that I would continue to panic. Is there another way?

A. A very good question and many people who have suffered from panic attacks often ask the same thing. The fact is though that you would have induced the head breathing voluntarily, under your own control, and since it is under your own control, then you will also be able to move the breathing further and slower down in your body too. You are learning to have control whereas people who have panic attacks know little about control.

Q. If I just learn the breathing exercise and breathing trances in this book, would that be OK?

A. It would certainly set you up for life but don't expect me to advise anyone to limit themselves. You know I know you are capable of so many things.

Q. I live next to a motorway. Should I really be deep breathing during rush hour?

A. Always check with your family doctor. Pollution is certainly one of the biggest problems to be solved by environmentalists (that means you too). Use a bike, drive your car less, lobby for electric cars, stop on the way to work by a field, or do your deep breathing indoors during daylight with a window open, where the carbon monoxide is reduced by indoor plants.

Further Reading

BHIKKHU, BUDDHADASA, **MINDFULNESS WITH BREATHING, A MANUAL FOR SERIOUS BEGINNERS**, WISDOM PUBLICATIONS, BOSTON, USA, 1988.

BRADLEY, DINAH, **HYPERVENTILATION SYNDROME: BREATHING PATTERN DISORDERS**, KYLE CATHIE, LONDON, 1991.

CARR, ALLEN, **THE ONLY WAY TO STOP SMOKING PERMANENTLY**, PENGUIN BOOKS, LONDON, 1994.

VERNY, THOMAS & KELLY, JOHN, **THE SECRET LIFE OF THE UNBORN CHILD**, WARNER BOOKS, LITTLE BROWN & CO, LONDON, 1981.

WELLER, STELLA**, THE BREATH BOOK**, THORSONS, LONDON, 1999.

YOGI RAMACHARAKA, **SCIENCE OF BREATH,** LN FOWLER & CO, LONDON, 1960.

Chapter Five

Eating Food for Life in the Temple

Ninety nine per cent of people in the developed world shovel garbage into their mouths more than 90 per cent of the time. Garbage literally means the stuff you would normally throw away. So there it is. If you are absolutely kind to your stomach, digestive system and nutritional needs you can go ahead and skip this chapter altogether; otherwise stay tuned.

One of the things I look at very closely when I assess a client's needs is what they eat, when they eat it, and how. Any doctor or therapist would be well advised to do the same because nutrition profoundly affects our health, thoughts, emotions, work, and ability to enjoy life. The majority of people who come to see me are unaware that part of their problem is that they are poisoning themselves with their diets.

All heathcare professionals can benefit their work by learning more about nutrition, but the truth is, most practitioners never ask their clients what they are eating, and if they know what effect that diet will have on their health. Most people are so detached from their basic nutritional needs in the western world that they are dying at alarming rates from blocked arteries, heart attacks, strokes and malnutrition. Yes...**MALNUTRITION** because regardless of the amount of food they are eating, that food has been so processed and denatured that a lot of the essential vitamins, minerals, fatty acids and proteins are lost. The foods they are eating have had much of the goodness extracted from them and destroyed in order to give the product a longer shelf life and a more sanitised appearance.

In the less developed countries the nutritional value of the food people eat is often far higher and diets are far healthier. They are not dying from the same kind of diseases as the populations of developed countries. We eat too much and particularly too much of the wrong kind of foods at the wrong time of the day. The most common reason we eat too much is because the products we are consuming are nutritionally deficient and the brain keeps telling us to shovel more into our mouths to satisfy our nutritional needs...**AND WHEN THE QUALITY OF FOOD INCREASES THE APPETITE DECREASES TO NORMAL.**

At school we are taught so many things but I have never encountered an educational programme that teaches children to look after their health in a holistic way when they grow up. Most of my generation grew up believing that if it is on the supermarket shelf it must be OK to eat. When I opened an organic hotel and restaurant in the mid 1980s people simply laughed, thinking I was ever so slightly crazy...now who's the crazy one?

Just recently a friend of mine from the English countryside came to stay with us in my flat right in the centre of London's West End. When talking about food he told me that where he lived it was much more difficult to buy organic food. Like you I found that quite ludicrous since he was in the middle of a field and I was next to one of Britain's busiest city roads.

Many of the foods we eat have had their molecules so dramatically altered by processing that they can be unrecognisable to the digestive system and are eliminated as waste. These bastardised molecules are also causing many people to be eating disease-inducing products without them knowing what they are putting into their mouths.

If the hydrogenation (chemical alteration) of fats to make margarine was invented today it would be doubtful it would get a licence. The only real oil you can generally buy in the supermarket is virgin cold pressed oil. Virgin oils need to be kept in dark glass, not exposed to air or light, and the oil extracted away from both to stop it going rancid. Go into your supermarket and look at all the clear glass bottles of oil with air pockets in the top because it will tell the tale that the manufacturer is often being less than honest with you on the label.

Oil manufacturers often say on their labels that nothing is added but they fail to tell you what was taken away in the heating, bleaching and deodorising of their products. What started as unsaturated fats can actually become just as harmful to you as saturated fats, found in animal products, by what is done to them by the manufacturing and heating processes, but do they put that on the label?

Agro-chemical companies wanting to introduce genetically modified (GM) crops have neglected to tell the public that their experimental crops have coincided with the mass deaths of butterflies. In India many of the crops Monsanto gave to farmers to try failed and left the farmers worse off than they had been with their traditional crops. But the real marketing trick was that, if you bought Monsanto's seed, you would have to buy its fertiliser to make it grow. Sounds like a great marketing double bind, doesn't it?

In 1999 the environmental campaigning organisation Greenpeace assessed surveys of the British public who overwhelmingly stated they did not want genetically modified food[1]. Experimental crops were pulled up in protest and the British government appeared to be representing the interests of the big chemical companies and was not listening to what the public wanted or did not want.

If the GM crops escape into organic fields by accident, organic farmers lose their accreditation. The wind blows seeds about, birds distribute seeds in their droppings and sooner or later we would all end up eating GM crops without any choice. Personally I do not want to eat tomatoes with fish genes spliced into them...***NEVER***.

There is enough good quality food in the world to feed everyone; it is just that it is hoarded in warehouses under the control of commodity dealers, who would rather let people starve than not make a fat profit. There is nothing wrong with the quality of the food we can grow, only the farmers and food retailers who hold it to ransom.

Many of the diseases that people suffer from today are because of bad diet and stress, and unfortunately the two encourage each other with people getting hooked into a poor health cycle. They do not mean for it to happen but they are concentrating so hard on surviving and getting as much out of life as they can that they lose sight of the basics.

The funny thing was that before I went organic I thought that I had lost some of my ability to taste as I grew up. Things never seemed to taste as exciting as I remembered them when I was small. But you do not have to believe that – in fact, I want you to prove me wrong if you can. Take an organically grown carrot and the supermarket plastic wrapped, fertilised, scrubbed equivalent...now taste them alternately. Don't stop there...do the same thing with celery...apples...cut an organic onion open and smell the difference.

If you think you have got it right by buying big supermarket chain organically marked produce you may be fooled. Some large manufacturers often use hydroponics to grow their vegetables and salads, which means that the produce can be grown largely in water and not in the soil in the ground. Although the produce is big and fat it does not have the mineral content that it would naturally draw up from the soil, therefore it is nutritionally deficient. You can often tell this has happened by the absence of taste in the product. Check with your local supermarket chain to find out how it grows its organic produce.

Fertiliser is a killer, no matter which way you look at it. Fertilisers are designed to kill organic matter, not by pulling up the weeds and strangling them, but by poisoning. So what do you think it will do to your insides?

And think about it guys, your sperm count is probably lower than your grandfathers, which is shame really because he did not get half the chances you get. It's not just the men who suffer from poor diets...women too...think about how many cancers you can pick from today and then look at the chemicals in processed, altered food that are known to cause them.

MY BODY IS A TEMPLE

I grew up in Britain's first post Second World War generation. It was a time of white bread, refined sugar, beef dripping, school milk, and enough toffee puddings to give you thunder thighs for life. All these things, our parents were told, were treasures of the promised land that went along with democracy and a new urban sprawl. What we have discovered since is that all that food was so processed and laden with saturated fats and monosodium glutamate (food additive) that if heart attacks and obesity did not get you, cancer would.

The reality of it all is that food, plain and simple, is the very best possible kind of nutrition we could hope for. Organic grains, pulses, fresh vegetables, legumes and fruit can give us all the nutritional carbohydrates, proteins, lipids, vitamins and minerals we need. Of course food takes so long to get to us nowadays, and because we do not just pluck it out of the ground, so many people are taking vitamin and mineral supplements which cost a great deal of money, manufactured by who...?

Add to that the stress of the artificial society we have created where people work unnatural amounts of time and are placed under a pressured life. See a nutritionist, talk to them, have blood tests, dietary analysis and take as many supplements as they and you think you need...but it won't do a bit of good if you eat junk food and garbage.

The food manufacturing and farming lobbies are huge. They have profound economic and political power as well as the ability to brainwash you with their advertising. The majority of them do not care whether or not you die from their produce in the long term, just as long as their short-term profit margins are as high as they can possibly make them. Think about their economic equations – what would be the profit margin of just digging things out of the ground compared with the highly processed food?

A lot of the cattle and dairy farmers were wiped out in Britain in the mid 1990s during the BSE (Mad Cow Disease) crisis, but the government refused to admit the full extent of the problem until other countries banned British beef. The French admitted feeding human and animal sewage to their livestock. It is well known that many birth defects are the result of the use of fertilisers on crops but in America the Federal Drugs and Food Administration (FDA), still supports the fertiliser manufacturers because their political power and profit is enormous.

One of the greatest hidden facts of nutrition is that human beings do not in any way whatsoever need to consume any animal, dairy or fish products. In fact the consumption of those products really causes more health problems than benefits people gain from eating them. However, just as petroleum companies bought out the patents and buried the electric car in the early 1900s, so do animal product farmers and processors spend a large percentage of their revenue on protecting their market share.

EVERYTHING I NEED NUTRITIOUSLY TO MAINTAIN AND PROMOTE LIFE GROWS IN THE GROUND OR FALLS OFF A BUSH OR A TREE

The human liver produces all the cholesterol we need in our bodies and still excretes excess. If anything, some people have a genetic disorder where they produce too much cholesterol. Animal-based food contains unnecessary cholesterol and saturated fats that block your arteries with poor nutritional content. Animal and fish products also contain prostaglandin E[2], a chemical that irritates arthritis and skeletal joint inflammation and dysfunction[2]. Would you pee in the petrol tank of your car?

Look at your teeth, then at the teeth of a cat or dog and see they are quite different; we are not natural carnivores. Then look at the teeth of gorillas and other vegetarian primates and you will see they have the same kind of dentures as ourselves. When have you ever seen a fully grown horse that eats anything but plants? Huge, strong, healthy gorillas don't eat cow or pig burgers, and their greatest threat to survival is humankind trying to produce more cow and pig burgers.

Meat eaters have a much greater risk of getting cancers – ask yourself why that is. They die sooner and of more preventable diseases than pure vegetarians (vegans).

Sometimes people say they are vegetarian but they eat white meats now and again. For those people, the truth is you are not being vegetarian. For people who eat fish – sorry no, fish have a spine and a face. Toxins are just as strong in dairy products if the cow has continually been fed large amounts of antibiotics and hormones. Some scientists believe the crippling digestive illness Crohn's disease is caused by bacteria in cow's milk[3]. The only creatures for whom cows' milk is good are baby cows.

RAW FOOD VEGANS...providing they are not eating hydrolysed or saturated coconut type fats are unlikely to have any form of arterial sclerosis, which means they rarely have heart attacks and strokes. Their greatest danger is more likely to be being knocked over by a cattle truck or dying of old age.

Sedentary lifestyles and eating animal products give rise to a much greater risk of colon cancer. Diabetics who used to be meat eaters find that many of them do not have to take medication anymore when they become raw food vegans[4]. Again ask yourself how the above could be true.

MY BODY CAN ALWAYS BE MY TEMPLE

Because farm animals are fed outrageous amounts of antibiotics and hormones to keep them free from infection and promote growth, people who eat those animals are also eating antibiotics. Like it or not this in turn is, through the food chain, over exposing meat and dairy eaters to a continual barrage of high level of antibiotics and artificially fed hormones. When those people are actually prescribed antibiotics for a medical emergency they find the drugs are often ineffective because the infection has grown so used to the high levels of antibiotics. Another problem is that the over-prescription of antibiotics for minor illnesses has led to the virulent mutation of viruses which have out-developed our present medicines.

The artificial hormones also change our physiology when people eat animals to whom the hormones have been fed. There is no escaping contamination through the mass farm animal food chain.

This also contributes to the creation of new auto-immune deficiency disorders such as ME, where the immune system, through stress and environmental toxins, just simply gives up one day. The stress on the body disables the white cells' adaptive immune system reactions against viruses.

WOULD YOU INJECT YOURSELF WITH MONOSODIUM GLUTAMATE (MSG)?

Due to environmental pollution, dioxins (by-products of agro-business and fuel emission) have got into the waters and fish now contain dangerous amounts. What is most frightening is that dioxin was a deadly by-product of Agent Orange, the poison that the Americans dropped on Vietnam. Dioxins are among the most carcinogenic substances on earth and here they are in liberal amounts in the food chain and governments are just trying to pretend they are not there.

I have an enormous number of people come to see me who work in the city of London suffering from the effects of working continually 16 hours a day, with no lunch or tea breaks and who only eat junk and fast food. The pattern is always the same – pale complexion, sweating, red in the whites of the eyes, fatigue, sleeplessness, panic attacks, lack of confidence, headaches, nausea and irritable bowel syndrome. Before they open their mouths I can tell what they are eating or not, how and when. The diagnosis is simple – their bodies are tired and their guts are complaining. They have disassociated from the needs of their bodies.

EAT ORGANIC

If you cannot afford the outrageous prices that some organic food stores charge, get an allotment and grow your own. The exercise will do your constitution and health more good than the money you earn working overtime. We are being conned by many farmers, dairy producers, food manufacturers, chemical companies, schools and governments. We are being ripped off...and they are making a great deal of profit out of convincing people to eat garbage and poison.

You are responsible for your own and your family's health. So, switch off the television adverts and read about nutrition. Question whether you need processed food at all, in which there are countless harmful hidden sugars, fats and chemicals. Then you will learn about the kind of nutrition the body really needs.

Even the wholefood stores are selling you breads, cakes and biscuits containing fats and sugars that have been altered by the cooking process that turns them into carcinogens and causes you to put on excess weight.

When people come to me with IBS, stomach problems, anorexia, nervousness, eczema, cancer, AIDS, and many other disorders, the first thing I ask them to do is to go onto a...**RAW FOOD VEGAN DIET**...cooking kills vitamins...Definitely do not take my word for it – go to your library and try to prove me wrong. When vegetables are cooked in water, many of the minerals are thrown away with it.

RAW ENERGY FOOD

Think about why you eat. List 10 reasons why you eat and then examine whether your present diet satisfies those needs. If all 10 are not satisfied then it is time for you to change. For many years people have thought of vegans or those who eat raw food as pale, thin, weak people who simply do not get enough protein...absolutely not true.

As a raw food vegan myself I am fitter, more alert, sleep deeper, full of energy, calmer, emotionally more stable and confident than I have ever been in my life.

HAVE YOU EVER SEEN AN EIGHT-FOOT GORILLA TRYING TO EAT A COW OR BOIL A PIG?

Let me ask you this...if you bought a new car, would you paint it a different colour, jab holes into it, cover it in grease, burn it with a blow torch and then leave it six months before you decide to drive it proudly down the high street on a Sunday afternoon? You would...my goodness you're crazy, there is nothing I can do to help you...If you would not, then think about what cooking and processing does to the nutritional content of your food before you eat it.

Organic raw food vegans who eat a balanced diet are the least likely persons to contract diseases. They are healthier, happier and more nutritionally satisfied than any other food group. I put ill or overweight people who come to see me immediately onto a raw food diet, with lots of nuts for protein, fruit and vegetables, and no processed garbage, as well as teaching them self-hypnosis.

AND WHAT DO YOU THINK HAPPENS?

Yes...they attain their natural weight and get better, as nature is able to extract its own medicine from their foods.

SHOP MORE, COOK LESS

Re-educating your eating habits is a learning curve and there are many publications to read which are listed at the end of this chapter. If you plan to live to 100 like me and intend to party all the way, think about how to eat yourself there.

Many people who have been raised in societies where there is mass manufacturing of confectionery suffer from mood swings due to the sugar buzz. Every time you open a magazine or switch on the television some big company is trying to sell their new candy bar that promises you heaven or as near as you can get to it for 50 pence or less.

Then there are confectioners of wedding cakes, birthday cakes, cream cakes and sometimes pure sugar compressed into suckable sweets. Billions of pounds all over the world are spent on convincing people to eat a whole lot of sugar they nutritionally do not need, which rots their teeth, makes them fat, and artificially elevates their moods, which naturally come crashing down later.

FRUIT CONTAINS FRUCTOSE (NATURAL SUGAR)

Your body can turn the carbohydrates, fats or proteins into glucose that can be burnt by your cells to produce energy. You do not need any added sugar in your diet. In fact added sugar only causes too much glucose to be present in your bloodstream that is transported as lipoprotein and then stored as excess fat in your adipose tissue until you need energy reserves.

Refined sugar from canes, beets, honey, and plants not only makes you fat, it also artificially confuses your emotions, and people who are used to having the sugar buzz can become very bad-tempered because to every up there is always a down.

Find someone you think has a sugar addiction and just watch them from a distance for a week and you will see what I mean. I also bet you that they probably will not see the sugar addiction as being related to their mood swings either and should you suggest it, they will vehemently defend their consumption.

Yes, we all have a sweet tooth, but nature provides us with absolutely fabulously sweet fruits in seasons which we can eat, preserve and dry. However, we have once again been brainwashed into believing that sticky desserts must follow starchy, fatty meals.

Since your gut can only digest certain kinds of food effectively at one time, it is much wiser to eat fruit at a different time than you eat protein, such as nuts. This enables your digestive system to focus on extracting the full nutritional value from each food as you eat it. This used to be referred to in America as the chemical diet but it is a hygienic way to treat your digestive system and allows maximum absorption of nutrients.

WAKE UP AND SMELL THE FOOD

A man came up to me at a talk I gave a few years ago and asked me if I could help his brother who was a policeman. The client came to see me because he was off work and had been in hospital with stress. During the initial consultation, because I always do a dietary analysis, I discovered that the man drunk several cups of coffee a day. When he stopped drinking coffee, black leaf tea, or sugared drinks his stress level went right down. After I taught him self-hypnosis he was able to go back to work straight away.

He really was not consciously aware of what he was doing to himself but the coffee drinking was something everyone did at the police station where he worked to stay awake during night duty.

Coffee can act like a laxative; it washes out the gut but prevents take-up of many vitamins and minerals. Black leaf tea contains tannin and caffeine, and can have a similar effect when drunk in copious amounts. It always amused me that during my childhood all the adults around me who had been in the Second World War marked every triumph, distaste, meal or break time with black leaf tea.

Coffee and black leaf cause people to be overtly nervous, edgy, moody and not in control of their emotional processes. People drink coffee and black leaf tea because they think it gives them energy, but it doesn't; it actually gives an amphetamine (speed) type high. Someone who ate with great care would have much more energy for far longer.

I CAN BE AWARE THERE ARE MANY KINDS OF ADDICTIONS

The most important advice I can ever give to an alcoholic or a drug addict is to get professional help – don't try to do it alone. Drug addictions can have many causes and you can get amazing help from doctors and therapists of many kinds who have helped thousands of people towards a great new kind of life.

Rather than recovering from chemical addictions, what can happen is that most individuals change into another kind of person, inducing a natural maturation, progress, growth and evolution. If the change of personality does not occur, the addiction remains, even if the person is in a state of abstinence.

COOKED FOOD IS AN ADDICTION

But it is one that has been passed down from generation to generation, the roots of which are no longer remembered. When humans left Africa and moved to colder climates there was often no time to plant and harvest crops so animals became the easiest form of food available. Dead flesh spoils very quickly and humans do not have the kind of teeth suited for tearing and devouring raw animal flesh (what does that tell you?) so flesh was cooked to make it more palatable.

Of course there is less profit for big businesses selling us naturally produced organic vegetables and fruit. The real profits for the corporations is processing the products as much as possible to make them so unrecognisable that we are unable to make them ourselves, therefore making them exclusive. In 1999 around 1 billion microwave ready meals were sold in Britain alone, so how much profit do you think that made the manufacturers? How many people do you know that have bought something and paid above the odds because they thought it was exclusive? Yes...you, and me too.

DRINK TO YOUR HEALTH

Nature has provided us with millions of plants of different kinds that produce leaves and flowers we can steep to have different kinds of therapeutic effects on our bodies. Camomile for headaches, ginger for digestion, peppermint for period pains, rosehip for vitamin C and blackcurrant to help with aching joints, to name but a few. Study them, buy a dozen boxes of assorted teas and keep them airtight until you drink for pleasure too.

Juicing is another great way to get natural nutrients in a concentrated form that will give you masses of energy and nutrition without having to eat too much bulk. Unfortunately pre-packed and treated juices lose much of their nutritional and vitamin content. Even when it says organic on the box it will still have been concentrated and then reconstituted, and in many places the makers will not even have to tell you. The only time it is really fresh is when it is squeezed before your eyes and even then make sure the produce is not older than the juicing machine. Go out and buy yourself a juicing machine or if you are short of money, invest in a manual juicer.

WATER...WATER EVERYWHERE

Our bodies are made up mainly of water which needs to be replenished constantly several times a day with a new supply of clean, fresh water just as if it were from a mountain spring. Nature provides as many chemicals as different types of minerals that leach out from mountains into clean, fresh water; some of these are beneficial to you and some are not. But never does nature produce water with chlorine in it, so why do governments need to add that to the water supply which reaches your home and then call it drinking water?

For dietary purposes we need six things: carbohydrates, fats (including oils), proteins, vitamins, minerals and water. Fresh fruits and vegetables contain all the carbohydrates you need. Nuts of many various kinds, sprouting pulses, oils, along with seeds give proteins and fats. Everything is made from amino acids, which are the building blocks of proteins, so everything you eat helps build proteins in your body.

If you learn about nutrition you will get all the vitamins and minerals you need for life in the uncooked food you eat. A few extra supplements, however, can help you cope with the pace of modern life but read up very carefully before you make them part of your regular daily routine. There are even different kinds of **RAW FOOD VEGANS**, such as fruitarians or people who live mainly on sprouts or pulses. You can be sure if they are eating a nutritionally balanced diet they will be much healthier, calmer, brighter and have more energy than omnivores, vegetarians, cooked food and junk food vegans.

LET FOOD BE YOUR MEDICINE AND MEDICINE BE YOUR FOOD (HIPPOCRATES)

Nutritionally aware raw food vegans generally have higher energy levels, less illnesses, colds or flu, lower bad cholesterol counts and higher good cholesterol counts, higher red and white blood cell counts and no nutritional deficiencies.

Going out to a restaurant as a raw food vegan with friends is not a problem. I always plan in advance and will maybe ring the restaurant to explain what I will want. Let's face it, if they have not got great raw ingredients in the first place, what are you doing eating there anyway?

Just recently I went to an academic medical conference and sat eating lunch among my colleagues who were psychiatrists, psychologists, therapists and surgeons. They had their courses of dead animal, dairy saturated fats and burnt offerings, and I coolly got out my lunchbox full of organic, raw plant food. There are always a few eyebrows and looks as if I am the one who is the crazy doctor, but who do you think had the healthiest meal?

Change your life by reading David Wolfe's **THE SUNFOOD DIET SUCCESS SYSTEM**. You will never look at food the same again as it will bring you back to the temple. Finally I shall teach you about food satisfaction. Your body produces enzymes that digest your food and the foods themselves also contain chemicals that link in with your body's chemistry to help digest food, releasing its goodness and nutritional content. When the natural chemical reaction happens in the raw state a signal goes to your brain which tells you that you are satisfied with the nutritional content of the food you have eaten. However, when food has been altered by heating or processing, then part of the signalling mechanism is distorted so you eat bulk, become stuffed, but are not satisfied. Nature knows exactly how to satisfy your chemical needs with plant foods in their natural state.

SMART DOCTORS WILL PRESCRIBE NUTRITION AS MEDICINE

Eating in the Temple (Script)
I can consider each day of my life...my body and I are one...**I LIVE IN MY TEMPLE WHICH IS A HOLY PLACE**...there have been times when this was

not so...but each day has been a learning curve...***AND I AM NOW PROUD TO BE THE TEMPLE KEEPER***...the gift of life is a sacred one...I can seek to appreciate its wonders...***I AM THE GUARDIAN...KEEPER...PRIEST OF THE TEMPLE***...food is the fuel with which I pay homage to the temple...only the very best is good enough for me...***I AM ENTITLED TO PURE...ORGANIC ...NATURAL FOOD***...no one has the right to ask me to eat less...I can strive to fulfil my needs for natural nutrition...***RAW FOOD GIVES ME THE BEST SOURCE OF NUTRITION***...fruit...vegetables...legumes...green leaves... grasses...nuts...seeds...berries are all I need...I can eat as many of those as I desire...***I CAN STUDY NUTRITION AND LEARN ABOUT ENERGY FOODS*** ...if others eat junk foods and garbage it is their business...I can take control over my own nutritional needs...***EATING CAN BE A PURE PLEASURE***...breaking the food addictions of the past gives me a whole new life...***I CAN GROW STRONG LIKE A GORILLA OR AN OX***...the sun's energy goes into the plants...then that energy can be transferred live directly to me...***I CAN BE THE RAW FOOD VEGAN PRIEST***...the priest who looks after the holy place in which I live...I can keep the temple pure and full of energy ...***THE FOOD I EAT WILL BE PURE***...considering each mouthful I put into my mouth...taking the time to chew my food 40 times before I swallow ...***KNOWING THAT FOOD IS VERY PRECIOUS JUST LIKE MYSELF***...I will respect my body and higher life forms...plants can be my staple diet...***I CAN BE FULL OF HEALTH...PEACE...AND NATURAL NUTRITION***...the food I eat will fill me with energy...and I will sleep deeply and peacefully...***I BECOME THE GOOD FOOD I EAT...THANKING IT FOR THE WONDERFUL HEALTH-GIVING NUTRITION***.

Going raw is a very gradual process that few people do all at once. What they tend to do is stop eating red meat first and then white meat, followed by cutting out fish. The next stepping stone is to change from dairy to soya products and eventually to raw food. Anyone who is raw will tell you that it is worth all the effort and that in many ways their lives have changed unrecognisably.

Use the various self-help raw food vegan groups that are around so that you can talk to the very people who have been through the detoxification stages that you will need to go through to be raw. There is much camaraderie and kindness among members of these groups and they will be quite happy to give you advice and tell you where fellow raw foodists are having meetings.

Do not expect non-raw food people to understand your dietary needs but instead think of it as an opportunity to teach them. Use the **Eating in the Temple** self-hypnosis script as part of your daily trance and start to make scripts up for yourself to suit each part of your transition to healthy eating...***BON APPETITE***.

EACH DAY I CAN EAT MYSELF BETTER AND BETTER DELIGHTFULLY

Summary
■ Learning as much as you can about nutrition and never accepting the propaganda fed to you by corporate food manufacturers which is designed to inflate the price of the product.
■ Consider your body as the holy temple in which you live for your entire life and respect it as priceless and invaluable to the living process.
■ Eat organic whenever you can, just as nature intended as it developed the body over millions of years.
■ Move towards a raw food vegan diet that will offer you greater chances of longevity and health than any other diet on earth.
■ Avoid chemicals, sugar, caffeine, tannin and addictions that arise from consuming processed and unnatural foods.
■ Reprogramme your mind to be excited about the good levels of constant energy that a well balanced raw food diet gives you without the ups and downs of manufactured, denatured products sold in shops.
■ Do the exercise on p167.

Frequently Asked Questions
Q. Doesn't being a raw food vegan (RFV) seem so extreme?
A. It is funny you should say that because I went to a party recently and thought exactly the same thing about the dead animal, old tinned vegetables, refined sugars, and denatured, processed and nutritionally deficient food they were serving. Your body is like your mind – what you put in governs, to a large extent, what you become.

Q. I have heard that vegans become lacking in certain vitamins and minerals. Is that true?
A. Some races and cultures, such as the Jains, have lived as vegans for hundreds of years to healthy and ripe old ages. There are so many myths put about by people who have not studied nutrition or who have a personal investment in disseminating the wrong information, such as animal farmers and a profusion of food manufacturers. Although many food producers mark their produce as organic, you need to remember that in the wild, crop rotation happens naturally.
The farmers from whom you buy your food need to be considering the way they farm organically so that the produce yields maximum mineral content, as well as a high level of vitamins. The answer is to examine your food and ask what it can do for you nutritionally as you study its contents and balance your diet. Raw food veganism is about thinking first and then eating.

Q. What do I do when people remark how bizarre they find my new eating habits?

A. *Thank them profusely for paying attention to your nutritional needs, then explain the whole RFV philosophy to them. You can plant the seeds of conversion if you wish but try not be a martyr or bore them.*

Q. *What do I do if I lapse and eat cooked food?*

A. *No one is perfect and some people lapse from time to time. There are people who are 95 or 90 per cent raw, particularly in the early stages of conversion, which needs to be a gradual process.*

Q. *Sometimes someone may have gone to a great deal of trouble to have cooked me a meal, so how do I deal with that?*

A. *Let it be well known that you are a RFV so no one is in any doubt or has any illusion.*

Q. *How long does it take to go raw?*

A. *It took me three months and several books to begin to understand what I was doing. It really happened properly when I eventually met other RFVs and we were able to share experiences, which taught me a great deal. I have never felt so good and have more energy than when I was 20 years old, which was quite a long time ago. Also, my mind is clear and calm.*

Using self-hypnosis I reprogrammed my eating habits, and my whole philosophy about food changed, moving towards an incredibly positive way of enjoying feeding myself with the best that can be available.

References

1. Attitudes Towards Testing Genetically Modified Crops (Impact on Organic Crops), Greenpeace, UK, June 1999.
2. Foods that Fight Pain by Dr Neal Barnard, pp104-105, USA, 1999.
3. Milk to Blame for Crohn's Disease?, Health Which? press release, London, 2000.
4. Physician's Committee for Responsible Medicine, news release, USA, September, 1995.

Further Reading

ARLIN, STEPHEN, FOUAD, DINI & WOLFE, DAVID, **NATURE'S FIRST LAW**, MAUL BROTHERS, CA, USA, 1996.

BARNARD, NEAL MD, **FOODS THAT FIGHT PAIN**, BANTAM BOOKS, LONDON, 1998.

BLYTHMAN, JOANNA, **HOW TO AVOID GM FOOD**, FOURTH ESTATE, LONDON, 1999.

BROTMAN, JULIANO, **RAW: THE UNCOOK BOOK, NEW VEGETARIAN FOOD FOR LIFE**, REGAN BOOKS, HARPER COLLINS, NEW YORK, 1999.

COLEMAN, VERNON, **ANIMAL RIGHTS, HUMAN WRONGS: A BLUEPRINT FOR A BETTER SOCIETY**, BLUE BOOKS, DEVON, UK, 1999.

DAVIES, STEPHEN & STEWART, ALAN, **NUTRITIONAL MEDICINE: THE DRUG-FREE GUIDE TO BETTER FAMILY HEALTH**, PAN BOOKS, LONDON, 1987.

DEAN, WARD & MORGENTHALER, JOHN, MD, **SMART DRUGS AND NUTRIENTS**, B&J PUBLICATIONS, CA, USA, 1990.

ERASMUS, UDO, PhD, **FATS THAT HEAL, FATS THAT KILL**, ALIVE BOOKS, CANADA, 1999.

GEAR, ALAN, **NEW ORGANIC FOOD GUIDE**, JM DENT & SONS, LONDON, 1987.

HANSSEN, MAURICE, **E FOR ADDITIVES: THE COMPLETE E NUMBER GUIDE**, THORSONS PUBLISHERS, NORTHAMPTON, UK, 1984.

LANGLEY, GILL, MA, PhD, MIBIOL, **VEGAN NUTRITION**, VEGAN SOCIETY, EAST SUSSEX, UK, 1995.

LEE, WILLIAM H, RPH, PhD, **THE BOOK OF RAW FRUIT AND VEGETABLE JUICES AND DRINKS**, KEATS PUBLISHING, CONNECTICUT, USA, 1982.

MILLER, SUSIE & KNOWLER, KAREN, **FEEL-GOOD FOOD**, WOMEN'S PRESS, LONDON, 2000.

WIGMORE, ANN, **THE SPROUTING BIBLE**, AVERY PUBLISHING GROUP, NEW YORK, 1986.

MABEY, RICHARD, **FOOD FOR FREE: A GUIDE TO THE NATURAL WILD FOODS OF BRITAIN**, PEERAGE BOOKS, LONDON, 1986.

MACKARNESS, RICHARD, **CHEMICAL VICTIMS**, PAN BOOKS, MANCHESTER, UK, 1980.

MARCUS, ERIK, **VEGAN – THE NEW ETHICS OF EATING**, MCBOOKS PR, USA, 1997.

MINDELL, EARL, **THE VITAMIN BIBLE**, ARLINGTON BOOKS, LONDON, 1979.

MUMBY, KEITH, **THE COMPLETE GUIDE TO FOOD ALLERGIES AND ENVI-RONMENTAL ILLNESS**, HARPER COLLINS, LONDON, 1993.

VAN STRATEN, MICHAEL, **SUPER JUICE**, MITCHELL BEAZLEY, LONDON, 1999.

WOLFE, DAVID, **THE SUN FOOD DIET SUCCESS SYSTEM**, MAUL BROTH-ERS, CA, USA, 1999.

Useful Organisations

Vegan Society, Donald Watson House, 7 Battle Road, St Leonard's-on-Sea, East Sussex TN37 7AA. Website http://www.vegansociety.com

American Vegan Society, PO Box H, Malaga, New Jersey 08328, USA.

Vegan Society of Australia, PO Box 85, Seaford, Victoria 3198.

Raw Health, 37b New Cavendish St, London W1M 8JR.

Fresh Network, PO Box 71, Ely, Cambs, CB7 4GU.
Website http://www.fresh-network.com

Chapter Six

Exercise Motivation

Many people go through life making excuses for not being involved with their bodies. They say they work too hard and do not have the energy left, are too poor to join a gym, have too many important things to do, have children that cannot be left, are too old, feel that the physical path is not really for them or find any excuses they can not to be responsible for their physical health.

When something goes wrong with their health they expect doctors to patch them up and return them to the kind of health they think they ought to have, yet they do not make an effort to physically promote that health themselves. This can, at times, be due to the fact that they may not be educated in the inextricable link between mind and body. Just like the very best Rolls Royce engine each part needs to be built and maintained with care, dedication and love.

It does not matter whether it is aerobics, jogging, swimming, callisthenics, circuit training, dance, martial arts, yoga or going to the gym, as long as you exercise regularly. Getting your quota of being at one with your body, which is, after all, the vehicle in which you travel through life, is part of the necessary integral human experience.

The benefits of regular exercise for any able-bodied individual are profuse, incorporating and promoting physical, mental and even spiritual well being. Some of you may already be aware of those benefits and take part in such exercise. However, we all have periods in our lives when we are unable to exercise in the ways that would give us benefits. Even if you are paraplegic, upper body exercise can substantially improve your sense of well being and happiness.

I PRESCRIBE EXERCISE TO MYSELF WEEKLY

I have been a very physical person in my life, enjoying athletics when I was young, being a professional dancer in my twenties and even going on to teach dance. What I remember about my physical life is that I performed better in many parts of my life as I was able to use my body to maintain a high level of total health.

What I will ask you to accept here is that...**LIFE IS AN INTEGRATED PROCESS**...and well being and social adjustment comes about when all our systems are working collectively. There is a caveat here though that there are a lot of people walking around this planet who have very high levels of physical health but who are not happy because parts of their brains are underused. I shall refer to these people as the *zombiefied fit* who take massive amounts of regular exercise but do not seem to realise the brain is a muscle too, and the more you use it the more its ability increases, helping you towards a satisfying life.

While society is prejudiced towards the body beautiful, with the fashion industry pushing anorexic pubescent girls down our throats, and Hollywood creating muscle men, not all of us can or want to match up to those unrealistic commercialised expectations. What we can do, however, is reach our own personal fitness best within the logical frameworks of our lives.

Responsibility for the Physical Self (Script)

I can let my body be an opportunity to express my physical best...twice or three times weekly exercise is sensible...***I CAN TAKE RESPONSIBILITY FOR MY PHYSICAL SELF***...generally I accept that frequent exercise helps good health...this can improve my physical...mental...and spiritual state of being...***I ACCEPT MY BODILY SYSTEMS ARE INTERCONNECTED WITH MY LIFE***...nature has taken million of years designing my body...in the wild I would exercise every day to gather food...***I BELIEVE PHYSICAL EXERCISE WILL PROTECT ME FROM DISEASES***...in the wild animals maintain maximum health through lifestyle...aim towards nature...emulating nature...and working with nature...***I WILL EXERCISE REGULARLY TWO OR THREE TIMES EACH WEEK TO MAINTAIN GOOD HEALTH***.

Exercise keeps muscle tone in good condition and helps the body support its organs so they can function at maximum levels of performance. This in turn helps the body attain a natural weight with enough fat stored for reserve energy in the adipose tissue just under the skin. Too much fat weighs the person down and causes a great deal of damage to the heart.

William had to have a kidney transplant at 22 as he had acute renal failure without warning. The doctors thought that it was due to him picking up an unusual virus in a foreign country. He had never really taken care of himself as during his teenage years he had drunk around six or seven pints of beer a night and smoked 20 cigarettes a day. Sport was not something he felt he had fitted into at school as he was more interested in being underneath a car with a box of spanners and an oily rag.

Fortunately for William his brother was able to donate a kidney and both of them survived. Scared and shocked by what had happened to him he decided to become a non-smoker, non-drinker and vegetarian, learned self-hypnosis, and took up marathon training under the supervision of his doctor. It just so happened that his general practitioner was a marathon runner who chose that sport to get away from the pressures of his work.

Together they trained every other morning and William became healthier and happier than he had ever been in his life. Within five years he won his first marathon and never looked back.

Not having too much fat allows organs to function at maximum tonality and capacity without unnecessary strain. Overweight people can have enlarged hearts which have developed to pump more blood around the extra tissue and this in turn weakens the heart and causes heart attacks.

Many people come to me for weight control guidance and as I take their histories they quite often tell me that they have been prescribed diet pills by doctors, with no mention of exercise. I have never yet met a client who has benefited in the long term from such medications. What tends to happen is that they lose weight for a time, become depressed, stressed, strung out and then put the weight back on, developing a vicious cycle. During exercise, particularly aerobic exercise, the adrenal gland produces hormones that assist in burning up the body's fat for energy, activating natural weight regulation.

Exercise has a particularly important effect on the gut in that it adds to peristalsis (the moving along of digestive products in the alimentary canal) which stops constipation. The gut is designed so that it extracts nutrition from the food and then expels the waste and poisons but during constipation the food debris stays in the gut too long. The poisonous substances that are not normally absorbed in the gut begin to leak through the gut wall into the body's systems if a person is constantly sedentary.

Earlier I talked about the importance of increased oxygen intake through good breathing which in turn can be promoted by cardio-vascular increase of the heart and lungs during exercise. Regular exercise helps use the maximum potential of the lungs so all the gases in the lower lung are exchanged, leading to the behaviour of deep breathing.

A very important thing to note about regular exercise is that it also promotes glandular production of hormones associated with excitation. This is excellent for dealing with depression where the body is stuck and not reaching the resolution and change stage of the behavioural cycle. Exercise is part of the best cure to break people out of depression, grieving and being stuck in the stress build-up state. Depressive states and psychological dysfunction have hugely reduced chances of surviving in a healthy body that takes regular exercise.

The immune and lymphatic system are also stimulated by regular exercise which helps a person's body guard against infection or disease. On top of that, someone who is diseased or ill is more likely to recover faster with more exercise because the body, as any doctor should tell you, often knows far better how to heal itself than any of our conscious minds and all our scientific knowledge put together.

What we need to do is give the body the opportunity to do the restoring and return to regulation of good health, called homeostasis.

Being Aware of the Body's Mechanics (Script)

I can be aware that my body has a self regulatory system called homeostasis...a system of self caring...repairing... and renewal...**I WILL USE MY EXERCISE TIME FOR THE PROMOTION AND BALANCING OF MY HEALTH**...the greatest medicine on the planet is self care...my mind can help take care of my body's self care...**I CAN THINK AND DO EXERCISE TWO TO THREE TIMES A WEEK FOR ONE HOUR EVERY TIME**...it's easy to allow that thinking to translate into reality...I will look forward to each of those exercise times...**I WILL SEEK THE EXERCISE TIME AS A SANCTUARY TO COMMUNE WITH MY BODY**...others may be present but my relationship with my body will be special...it can be an exclusive physical experience...**I WILL FEEL ELATED AT BEING ABLE TO FEEL DIFFERENT PARTS OF MY BODY OF WHICH I AM NOT NORMALLY CONSCIOUSLY AWARE**.

There are people who are too fanatical about exercise and can do it once a day or more continuously. Unless you are a professional athlete or dancer this is quite unnecessary to maintain good health. One of the problems that can arise with such regularity for a great many people is that it can wear out the joints and cause physical damage. If you look at old dancers or athletes you see that they often hobble around where they have seriously overworked their bodies and incurred a great number of injuries over their lifetime.

With too much physical exercise, hormonal changes also affect the ways the body is working and men can become very edgy and aggressive as their testosterone level moves extraordinarily high. Women's periods can stop as they become overtly muscular and masculine looking, growing body and facial hair. While the periods are likely to start again after those women have ceased exercise, some of the masculinisation may not necessarily be reversed, although the hair can be removed by laser treatment.

When someone is motivated to do too much or little exercise, one of the things that doctors look at is thyroid dysfunction. An underactive (hypothyroid) thyroid may mean a person is very lethargic and they may need supplementary medication. Others may have too much thyroid activity (hyperthyroid) and may feel as if they are constantly bombarded with unexplainable hyper behaviour. Both conditions need to be checked out by a medical doctor along with signs of anaemia where the red blood count is low and the person feels very run down.

There are also people who suffer from what is called Body Dysmorphic Disorder who, no matter what happens to their body, greatly dislike and even detest its form. Such people need professional help and should seek the care of a therapist, psychiatrist or psychologist who specialises in that field and not try to handle the situation on their own. Often they are trying to work through issues that may actually be nothing to do with their bodies but that is the medium they are using to have control over their lives. Such a condition may also be due to physiological dysfunction because of chemical imbalances.

If you are a person who has not been used to physical exercise, either through having been a white collar worker, had a couch potato lifestyle, having been at home with children, or because of illness, there is always a need to start slowly and build up your routines under the guidance of a professional instructor. Perhaps apathy or fear of failure may have been one of your mindsets in the past but you can get over this as you take your body in your hands and begin to work with it as its friend.

FALLING IN LOVE WITH YOUR BODY is one of the most essential parts of having exercise as part of your regular routine. In today's hierarchical body perfect commercialised class system we constantly get messages that tell us we are not OK. The reason the corporate sector spends trillions of pounds, dollars and yen (eventually the world dollar) every year giving those subliminal messages to us is because they want to sell us products to make us believe that they will make us OK. And of course they are making a great deal of profit out of suggesting misery to us and then selling us a cure for their suggested deficiencies.

So many people in this world are desperately unhappy and dissatisfied with their bodies, being at war with them and not in love with themselves. Many religions talk about the sin of self-obsession but I have to tell you this work is all about self-obsession because how else can you lay the foundations to become a whole person and then have the strength to help others? To be a whole person you need to put your own house in order first and keep checking that it is in order – now replace *house* for *body*.

The 20th century suffered from the legacy of psychologist Sigmund Freud, whose ideas became enshrined in our cultures. Among other things, he wrote about the Narcissus complex. This is where a person is in love with themselves and Freudian philosophy pathologised that behaviour. Well, I say to you...**FALL IN LOVE WITH YOURSELF OVER AND OVER AGAIN**.

Doris was at least 20 stone when she came to see me and since I never keep scales in my office we did not weigh her. At school she had been teased mercilessly about her size as she had always been an overweight child, unhappy at home, sexually abused by her father and referred to in the village that she lived as DD (short for Double Doris). She put up with the nickname because it was preferable to what she thought was the old-fashioned name that her mother had chosen for her.

As a child she had hidden to get away from the teasing, becoming her own playmate and making up stories for herself. She was painfully shy but at just 22 managed to get a job as an editor for children's story books. At work she felt like the odd one out because, not only was she the only virgin in the office, she was also the only one without a boyfriend to talk about.

The reason she came to see me was because she wanted to learn to lie effectively so she could talk about boyfriends with the rest of the staff who were all under 30. I made a deal with her that I would teach her to lie effectively if she agreed to go on a raw food diet, learn self-hypnosis and take regular exercise three times a week under the supervision of a personal trainer. Each month Doris lost approximately 14lbs until she hit 10 stone when she became the sub-editor of a fashion magazine, moved in with the men's editor, and bought a lap-dog whom she called Mable.

Since we are all individuals with an enormous amount of different factors affecting our lives it would be arrogant of any of us to presume that we are superior to others just because of our body form. Some people are whiteish, blackish, brownish, tallish, shortish, thinish or biggish. To discriminate against someone because of their body type or particular physical features is what is called *body fascism* and totally unacceptable in any democratic civilised society.

I have been involved for many years in civil rights movements that educate, fight against discrimination, and lobby for legal reform in the fields of sexism, racism and body fascism, so when I write this I am not only passing on my knowledge but also my philosophical beliefs. I have seen many people who have suffered ridicule, oppression, prejudice, denigration and just plain cruelty for having their particular body type. Often the people who perpetrated those aggressive, offensive prejudices against the suffering individual did not have any idea about the misery they were creating...but I must say to you that in law, ignorance is no excuse.

We all have a duty in a humanistic world, which eventually will be the only way we will survive as a species, to regulate our own prejudices against others. However, what is often forgotten is that we also have a duty to guard against prejudice and against taking part in that prejudice. In a perfect world this would not happen but we do not live in a perfect world. So we must constantly correct that by improving our internal self-images of ourselves and strengthen our positive images of others too that have been eroded by the reality of life.

Creating Body Well Being (Script)

I can progressively through my life review my body self image...I accept that perfection is an illusion...***I AM ACCEPTABLE AND LOVEABLE TO ME***...the reality of life is that exercise is a natural weight control and health promoter ...it is incontestable in that medicine has studied millions of individuals' health...***I CAN STUDY MY HEALTH...BODY AND WELL BEING...ON A DAILY BASIS***...each week I can put time aside for myself...exercise is important in my routine...***I CAN LOVE MY BODY AS IT IS PRESENTLY***

...taking stock of my physical self I can take steps to maintain the health I have...I can also take steps to improve aspects of my physical self...*I CAN VISUALISE THE IMAGE OF MY FORTHCOMING SELF*...to that it is easy to add sounds...feelings...tastes...smells...multiplying that imagery by six ...each image can produce a stronger association to the new me...*I JUMP INTO THE FIRST IMAGE AND EXPERIENCE THAT GOOD REINVENTION OF MYSELF*...changing the physical components to make that the strongest element for a while...adjusting each aspect of the components of experience ...*I JUMP INTO THE SECOND IMAGE OF MYSELF BECOMING MORE STRONGLY ASSOCIATED TO THE MORE PHYSICALLY HEALTHY ME*... fingers...toes...ears...nose...muscles...bones and every part of my physical self...it's easy to love my ability to have control over my own body...*I JUMP INTO THE THIRD SELF MORE STRONGLY ASSOCIATED WITH MY EVER POSITIVE CHANGING SELF WHO DOES REGULAR EXERCISE*...adaptability is the key to physical excellence...no one can ever stay the same and it is good to be able to utilise that...*I CAN JUMP INTO THE FOURTH POSITIVE IMAGE OF MY HEALTHY EXERCISING SELF*...exercising time can be a sanctuary...free from telephones or any interference from others...*JUMPING INTO THE FIFTH STRONGER POSITIVE IMAGE OF MYSELF OWNING PERPETUAL CHANGE*...the first person with responsibility for my health is me...as a mature person I can accept those things...*FINALLY JUMPING INTO THE SIXTH POSITIVE HEALTHY EXERCISING SELF I CAN OWN AND LOVE MY BODY*.

Psychosomatic Memories

Sometimes people have what are called somatic memories which is when an incident in the past is remembered by the brain and installed as a certain physical characteristic. This can be interpreted in many ways as short sightedness, partial deafness, gastrointestinal problems, irritable bowel syndrome, a limp, painful joints, muscle fatigue, back ache, phantom pain (imagining pains that are not really there), breathlessness, heart pains, high blood pressure, and skin disorders.

The emergence of such symptoms should always be checked out by a medical practitioner; however, the cause of such chronic symptoms often cannot be found. What tends to happen is that doctors over-prescribe medications that can become addictive. We call these memories psychosomatic in that they are both psychological and physical.

Many years ago when I was at college I would sit with the other students in a corner table and watch the people coming into the canteen to try to read their body language, discovering aspects of their histories and lives. Every lunchtime a teenage girl would collect her lunch on a tray and ever so slightly limp towards a table by the door where her girlfriends would sit.

After a month of watching her we wagered between ourselves why it was she ever so slightly limped. Among the collective explanations we came up with were ligament damage, one leg shorter than the other, rickets, neurological disease, in-growing toes nails and blisters.

When we eventually interviewed her and asked her about the limp, she had no conscious awareness that she was walking in that particular way. What we did find out was that three years previously, when she was at school, her family were poor and unable to afford new shoes for her. The older sister gave her some boots for the winter which had a nail sticking up inside. Because her mother and father were so stressed by the poverty-stricken situation the girl never told them about the nail, afraid that they would not be able to afford to buy her new boots. The memory of how she had to walk all that winter to avoid the nail had stayed with her as an expression of her physical movement.

Most people are unaware that they are able to change so much about themselves, including the way their body works, by the control and reprogramming of their minds. It is, I think, in many ways contrary to the idea that only doctors can change the way the body works through chemicals or surgery. These ideas have been sold to the general public for the past 150 years since surgery came out of the barber's shop and apothecaries were, to a large extent, replaced by international global chemical corporations, who will do virtually anything to protect their market share of the pharmaceutical business.

Medicine and surgery do wonderful things within the larger confines of medicine but they are overused and the client is constantly disempowered, giving responsibility for their health far too often to healthcare professionals for far too long. I guess here you might think I am talking my colleagues and myself out of a job, and in many ways I am, but I am a brief therapist who believes in minimal intervention. It is the best approach to quickly hand the responsibility for the client's health back to the client.

So to get a person who has psychosomatic blockages back into actualising their health and exercising well, it is necessary to deal with that unprocessed information. If these memories are serious, I would suggest consulting a hypnotherapist who specialises in sports programming and reprogramming.

Removing Memories of Physical Injury (Script)

I can be aware in my head of a time when I incurred a physical injury...it is possible to consider that I may still be hanging onto the memory of that injury...***I CAN ALLOW THE MEMORY AND ITS EFFECTS TO COME TO MY CONSCIOUS AWARENESS***...what I can also be aware of is that the memories which hold back my performance may be mental or emotional ...everyone is a combination of all of those things...***MY UNCONSCIOUS CAN ALSO MOVE THOSE MEMORIES FORWARD TO RESOLUTION CREATING CHANGE***...my unconscious has all the time it needs to do those things inside my head...there is no subjective rush or hurry...***MY CHANGE CAN HAPPEN QUICKLY IN REAL TIME TO FREE MY BODY***...there may be things that my conscious mind cannot understand or know how to deal with...however my unconscious has the ability to deal with those memories at many levels...***I CAN LET GO OF THE RESIDUE OF THOSE OLD UNNECESSARY MEMORIES***...it's all right for my body to change and become more fluid...active...and with all the systems working in synergy ...***MY UNCONSCIOUS ALREADY KNOWS WHAT TO DO SO I CAN ALLOW IT TO DO ITS JOB NOW!***

Hypnosis has often been used to improve physical performance with athletes, not only under the name of self-hypnosis but also sophrology, autogenics, visualisation and other mind control techniques not mentioned here. During the time before glasnost in Russia a lot of money and research was put into training the country's athletes in self-hypnosis to increase their performance and if we look at the results they achieved between the 1950s to the 1980s we can how excellent they were. The famous golfer Tony Jacklin was well known for his visualisation of a shot before he actually made it.

Different things are happening when hypnosis is used to increase performance levels in sport when it is used before the event. First, the internal experience of going through the action in your head, in advance, takes away the stage fright from the event because you have already gone through it in your own virtual reality in advance. Athlete Roger Bannister had problems trying to break the four-minute mile record but once he learned mind techniques to do it in advance of the event he reached his goal.

Second, it enables the person to install a sense of calm and pre-thought out judgement concerning the sports event they are about to perform. This gives the ability to change, alter, and re-evaluate the situation in advance of the actual performance. This feedback mechanism about the performance takes place before the performance and is very self-enlightening.

Third, because you have succeeded at the event in your head beforehand, you have the confidence to go ahead and perform to the best of your ability during the actual event. People who do not use mind techniques generally do not have as much confidence to perform as they are unaware of the outcome but those who practise mind techniques have imagined the success in advance.

Fourth, the ability to focus to the exclusion of distraction during the event grows as a person learns to train their mind as well as their body. If we look at weightlifting contests we can see that it is often not the person with the biggest muscles who wins but the person with the best rehearsed technique...and undoubtedly technique comes from the mind first.

Jamie was a student in her third year at university doing well and compet-

ing in karate competitions for which she trained three times a week. Her university studies were going well and she had no financial problems because she was still living at home with her parents. Although she was a black belt she said that she felt she had somehow reached the limit of her achievements in karate and there was a barrier that was stopping her winning the competitions for which she was putting herself forward.

When we talked about her life and schedule she discovered that in many ways she was spreading her attentions around in too many directions, and although she could achieve good results in all areas, excellence would require a more focused approach in a singular direction.

She learnt self-hypnosis with a particular attention to sports hypnosis that she practised every evening along with a new schedule of karate training. When she finished university she took a year out before work and was sponsored by a company to go into international competition in which she was very successful.

It does not matter if you are a mum who wants to get back into the exercise routine after having a baby or a top-class world athlete, the process is exactly the same to motivate your excellent physical performance.

Experiencing Physical Excellence (Script)

In wanting to be able to achieve my physical goals I can think...although I have reactions my mind can reprogramme my actions...***I CAN INSTALL NEW CONCEPTS OF MY ABILITY TO PERFORM PHYSICALLY***...seeing the goal in my mind visually can give me a clear place to aim...adding to that sound...feelings...taste...smell...***I CAN IMAGINE HOW I AM WHEN I HAVE ACHIEVED THAT GOAL***...examining how I stand...look...speak...think...how elated are my internal feelings...experiencing that marvellous sense of achievement and all its elements...***I CAN REMEMBER THE TOTAL EXPERIENCE OF SUCCESS AND TAP INTO IT WHENEVER I WANT***...being aware what it is like to have that success...giving that experience of success an identity...***I CAN BE AWARE THAT SUCCESS OF HAVING ACHIEVED WILL BE WITH ME DURING THE ACTUAL JOURNEY***...my personal best is the only prize I need for my efforts...and those efforts I can experience with sincerity and personal prestige...***I CAN FOCUS ON THE TASK IN HAND DURING MY ACTIONS***...the rest of the events of the world do not need to be remembered for a while...forgetting the other things in my life as I focus ***...ALL MY ENERGIES I BRING TO BEAR ON MY PHYSICAL EXCELLENCE*** ...I will see...hear...feel...taste and smell only the task in hand...for a time until the physical task is over nothing else will matter...***MY ATTENTION WILL SOLELY BE BROUGHT UPON ACHIEVING MY GOAL***...this is a time to rehearse the whole task in my mind as if seeing it on a cinema screen ...evaluating my performance and changing what needs be...***I TAKE***

CONTROL OF MY PHYSICAL...MENTAL...AND SPIRITUAL SELF THAT HELPS ME COMPLETE THE TASK WITH A SENSE OF EXCELLENCE...as I prepare for and start that task the excellence will come to me again... courage to be my best can be a joy to me...*UNTIL MY TASK IS OVER I WILL FOCUS ON IT AND CONCENTRATE WITH GREAT PLEASURE EXPERIENCING PHYSICAL EXCELLENCE*.

Summary

■ Treating physical exercise as part of a whole life-integrated living system that maintains and promotes health and a sense of excellence.

■ Organising time management so that your time with your body is sacred and there are no interruptions or disturbances from people, telephones or anything at all.

■ Falling in love with your body and treating it like royalty to be adored and looked after to the highest standard.

■ Becoming inspired to serve your body's need for exercise two to three times a week by installing motivation in trance.

■ Clearing any old memories of previous injuries or physical difficulties so the body and mind can accept new programmes to go to the next level of personal physical excellence.

Frequently Asked Questions

Q. With the pressure of work, children, paying the mortgage, and keeping everyone else happy, how can I find time to exercise?

A. Without time for your own needs you have no life as you are just a servant to everything and everyone else, having given every piece of yourself away. Get a life, as the Americans say. Let your diary be your best friend and let it co-operate with you in a programme of self-care. If you are in good condition you are giving good vibrations out to other people as well as to yourself.

Q. With someone like me who is naturally fat, would regular exercise really make such a difference?

A. There are very few people who suffer from glandular disorders or illnesses which cause them to be obese. By far the majority of people who are overweight are that way because they have acquired habitual over-eating patterns. No matter who you are, unless your doctor expressly advises against it, exercise, combined with diet, reinforced through hypnosis, will help you attain a natural and comfortable weight and size.

Q. How important is the hypnosis element of the programme?

A. Essential because suggestion motivates action and the suggestions you make to yourself during self-hypnosis give you the correct mindset to get the correct body for you. Your mind runs your body. So what kind of mind is run-

ning your body?
If you want to change your body, change your mind.

Further Reading
ALEXANDER, TANIA, **NO SWEAT FITNESS**, MAINSTREAM PUBLISHING COMPANY, EDINBURGH, UK, 1992.

DEVEREUX, GODFREY, **DYNAMIC YOGA**, HARPER COLLINS, LONDON, 1998.

LEIBOWITZ, JUDITH & CONNINGTON, BILL, **THE ALEXANDER TECHNIQUE**, HARPER & ROW, NEW YORK, 1991.

MITCHELL, DAVID, **THE COMPLETE BOOK OF MARTIAL ARTS**, CHANCELLOR PRESS, LONDON, 1989.

SHORTT, JAMES, **SELF DEFENCE: THE ESSENTIAL HANDBOOK**, SIDGWICK & JACKSON, LONDON, 1984.

Chapter Seven

Overcoming the Negative *Me* Diseases

We discussed earlier how voices and images inside your head could change the way you think. Positive voices and images identify possibilities and affirm abilities in the present and the future, moving a person into the **ACTIVE** mode of behaviour. Negative voices, however, set up patterns in the mind that prevent things from happening and people are more likely to move into the **REACTIVE** mode of operating.

Fully learning to recognise the differences between the *active* and *reactive* modes of operating is the key to being able to switch from one to the other whenever necessary to take control of your life. Here I am not saying that one is eminently superior to the other but certainly if you want to change things in your life then you undoubtedly need to move into the active mode.

The reactive mode of operating does, however, have its role in our life because most importantly it is part of our defence mechanisms which operate our reflexes. When we step on a nail or realise that we are in a dangerous or uncomfortable situation it is our reflexes that rescue us by withdrawing the foot to safety. At the times when we are being reactive, when it is not appropriate, we are doing that out of habit rather than good judgement.

There are many *me* diseases that form into negative mindsets and thought patterns that help detract us from good living experiences and wellness. In this chapter we are going to look at a few; however, I want you to begin to recognise when you are doing a *me* disease by examining your own thoughts.

From time to time, stop in the middle of a behaviour, write down the thoughts that you think drive the behaviour you are performing. Then look to see if your thoughts and actions will really get you to the goal that you originally set out to achieve before you started your present behaviour.

If you are getting good results with that behaviour, all is well. On the other hand if you never seem to achieve what you set out to, it is more than likely that you are too negatively subjective in your thinking, and are performing a *me* disease. The answer is to redesign the messages you are giving to yourself into **POSITIVE ACTIVE** content and context, instead of **NEGATIVE REACTIVE.** You will get the hang of it as you go through this chapter.

The *Why Me?* Disease

This is a loop behaviour that plays the same phrases and images over and over again inside your head. Millions of people in the 20th century spent fortunes on lying on the couches of psychoanalysts trying to get to the bottom of why things have happened to them or why they are like they are. One of the big dangers with this disease is that eventually it finds someone to blame for the kind of dilemma in which people believe they find themselves.

Although blaming has a social purpose in that it is part of the shaming system that holds each and every citizen to account for their actions, it does not in the long run give solutions to unhappy situations or personal troubles. Since life is so complex and we have so many experiences, the real answer to who is truly to blame for all our problems can never be found. Therefore it is unlikely the answer to the Pandora's box of a question of *why me*? can ever be found and it will continue in its diseased way to go around and around in a person's mind, driving them increasingly crazy and tortured.

This mind loop can have further negative sub voices that go:

Me, me, why poor little me? Why does this always happen to me? What did I ever do to deserve this? It does not happen to other people like it happens to me. Oh, why, why me?

Many long-term neurotics have this voice circulating in their heads. The answer that they are generally given by the psychiatric system is take a pill and if that does not work, take another one. The problem with this approach is the voices do not go away but simply go deeper into the unconscious and are no longer heard at a conscious level. Nevertheless the voices still cause a person to feel helpless, depressed, and oppressed. The psychiatric system can often mislabel people with these voices inside their heads as chronic depressives, paranoid, neurotic, troublesome, unco-operative, and hopeless cases.

What I want you to realise is that in order to move on in your life it is not absolutely necessary to answer the question *why me?* Yes, it can be useful to know why something happened so that, if it was a bad thing, you could avoid such a thing happening again, but it is not absolutely necessary to know the answer to carry on comfortably with life. It can also be useful to know what the trigger was if the happening was a good thing so that you know how to make it happen again.

The question *why me?* is a naturally occurring thought that comes just before another stage of thinking that leads to resolution. The next natural step is *Do I want to experience that again or not?* If the answer is *yes* then the experience is likely to have been an enjoyable one so no disturbance of the mind would have occurred. When the answer is *no*, with part or all of the experience being unpleasant and contrary to well being, then simply avoiding that situation in the future can suffice to keep a person safe.

As I write this I can hear some psychotherapists out there say: *Oh but people must know why things happen to them so that they can come to terms with what has happened.* My simple answer is that it is not always necessary and you should look at what investment you have in your clients coming back again and again each week.

Just the other day I came into my office and found that all the telephones had stopped working. I was annoyed because I had planned a busy morning with my secretary catching up on all our administration and phone messages. What's more there was a pile of faxes to send to confirm lecturing and teaching dates. When I went out into the street to investigate the annoying noise of drilling, the telephone company man had dug a big hole and was holding what looked like a bunch of a couple of thousand different coloured small wires in his hand.

"Excuse me please," I said. "Do you know how long it will be before my telephones are back on again?" He looked at the thousands of wires and then at me and smiled, saying: "If you are a red wire then probably 15 minutes, but if you are a yellow or green wire then at least an hour." This was all the information I needed to know to carry on with my morning constructively. What the difference was between the colours was not important to me. I did not want a course in electronics, or to find out if he was going to do the yellow or green wires first because as a person waiting for the telephones to come back on this would have served no purpose.

Sometimes people make life too difficult for themselves. They do not intend to do that, it is just that no one ever taught them to take the short cuts around trouble and instead they get stuck in the trenches like the *why me?* disease.

Jean Paul Sartre once wrote: "Life is what you do with what happened to you", but I would shorten that even further, cutting it back to the simplest equation:

LIFE IS WHAT I DO WITH WHAT HAS HAPPENED

What I am not saying is that you must forget the bad things that have happened to you in your life, because each thing that happens teaches you lessons. But you do not have to keep going back into the faulty loop of asking *why me?* when the answer may be too complicated for your conscious mind to understand. Move on to the next stage of learning, watching out for the same dangers again, if they were unpleasant, then avoid them and experience the next adventure.

The *But* Disease

People really have no idea that they are doing the *but* disease and that they are often negating the positive things they say by putting negative linguistic disclaimers in the middle of their sentences. So much of the positive content of the first part of the sentence is disqualified by the second part of what becomes a compound two-part sentence.

A typical example of this would be my friend's father who recently went on a day trip to the seaside. It was a day out that he had been looking forward to

*for a long time. When asked how his day out had been he said it was won-
derful going out with all his mates but the bus had been too hot. Asked how
the lunch had been he said it was very nice but he did not like foreign food. His
neighbour asked him if the trip had been value for money and he replied yes,
but it was too much money for one day.*

The *but* disease becomes a habit that operates out of conscious awareness
on automatic pilot and can make people very unhappy with their lives. They
feel that they never quite get to a state of well being and happiness. Somehow
that is always just out of their reach and they never quite know why they are
not having a fulfilling and rewarding living experience.

*Petunia came to see me at my office for hypnotherapy and she told me how
she believed in hypnosis and then asked: "But what if it does not work?" She
said that she had plenty of money to afford private treatment but that money
was tight. When I asked her if she wanted to get well again she answered:
"Yes, but what if I don't get well? But what if it is not really getting well but I
am only pretending?"*

The answer and solution to the *but* disease is so simple that people often
find it difficult to believe at first. For the *but* to exist there must be more than
one part to the sentence or thought. Replace the *but* (throw the *but* in the bin)
with an *and*, turning the second half of the sentence or thought into a positive statement.

With thoughts and statements, keep the affirmations in the second part of
the sentence in the first person singular so that your inside voice is talking
about you and empowering you, for example:

I have been diagnosed with cancer but what if I never get better? turns into:
*I have been diagnosed with cancer and I can find ways of living that include
trying to be as well as possible.*

Another way of dealing with the *but* is to add on more parts to the sentence
or thought, using more *ands*, building more positive constructs, for example:

I love my wife but I am not her perfect partner turns into: *I love my wife, and
that is a good feeling, and it is interesting for us to discover new ways in which
we can build an even better relationship.*

I CAN BUILD ON MY SUCCESSES TIME…AND TIME…AND TIME AGAIN

As a hypnotist when I use the word *but* it is cautiously, not excessively. We
are looking at creating constructive thoughts, not destructive ones.

The *If Only* Disease
I remember my Aunty Gwen, who each time we walked down the lane past a

very large new bungalow, would say: "I used to go out with the man who owns that bungalow before he was rich. If only I had married him I would be living there."

Each winter as her son was pulling sheep out of the ditches in the snow Aunty Gwen would comment: "If only you had gone to university like your brother you would not be doing what you are doing." Every time we drove up the lane to the farm where she lived with my Uncle Jack, she would repeat: "If only your Uncle Jack had not bought this farm, I would not have to do so much work."

I did not go to Aunty Gwen's funeral after she got run over by a bus, because I had moved a long distance away, but I can guess what noises I would have been hearing from the coffin.

Some people spend their whole lives wishing they were or had been somewhere else. Such people very rarely do anything to change their circumstances in order to make things different but they do continually construct an *if only* scenario inside their heads that always presumes the grass is greener on the other side of the fence.

A healthy, flexible mind seeks to change the circumstances that a person finds themselves in if things are not good or right for them. An unhealthy approach is to suffer and then complain about those circumstances without doing anything about them.

The *if only* disease denigrates the life experience that the person is having at that moment and always presumes that another path would have produced dramatically better results. Well it is true that under certain circumstances that might be so but in general we have to deal with the lives that we are living now to improve our present lot. In the discipline of Neuro Linguistic Programming (NLP), which is a form of hypno-psychotherapy, there is a saying:

IF WHAT I AM DOING IS NOT WORKING...DO SOMETHING DIFFERENT

Many people make excuses for themselves by forming thought patterns that say I am too old, uneducated, married, poor, ethnic, religious, weak or committed to my family. This excuse can formulate as being anything that serves the purpose of being an excuse. The excuse serves a purpose of keeping the person in the same circumstances as they are complaining about because they perceive it as being safer to stay where they are than to take a leap into new circumstances. They are afraid of change, even though they are complaining that they are not comfortable at the moment.

A little tape runs at a deep unconscious level that says *the danger you know is better than the danger you do not, so let's stay in the uncomfortable place and suffer the danger you know.* They also have another tape that says *well if*

I had done the other thing my lot would have been better.

We each have our own individual life course for whatever reason that happens. To continually complain that your life might have been better is setting yourself up for failure. It is a fruitless exercise that sabotages your life strategies in the present and future since you will be undermined by a strategy of not coming to terms with the reality you are living. It also denigrates the decisions you have made in the past. So the *if only* is not just minor griping as it is fundamentally damaging to your life pattern. A better strategy to adopt would be:

This happened to me...so what can I learn...***I CAN IMPROVE MY LIFE BY THE KNOWLEDGE I HAVE GAINED***...I accept my life course...I can develop more power over the choices I can make...***I GAIN CONTROL NOW AND IN THE FUTURE***.

The *Not Me* disease

This is abdication of responsibility for the self and others around you. People do not necessarily set out to be in denial about their responsibility for life but they can get caught up in the momentum of a decision that leads them down the cul-de-sac from which they have problems escaping.

I think we also have to remember that much of our society is based on mottos and deceptions that are part of the cultural norms. Some of those ideas state:

It's a shame about the environment but my little bottle of bleach won't make much difference.

I know you are dying of cancer so me having just one cigarette at your bedside won't hurt you.

Why should I get involved with politics when it doesn't affect me?

It's unfortunate you got beaten up but I don't see what difference my witness statement will make – besides I may get the sack for testifying.

Let the government pay me social security because those rich people have got plenty of money and they won't miss it.

It's been a terrible life but I blame my parents, not myself.

While thinking about the big picture, people are often prone to circumstances that are beyond their control like war, violence, bigoted persecution, child abuse or economic collapse. There is much, however, you can take responsibility for creating or changing in your life. For the most part, life is not in the hands of the gods, as far as I know, but a series of opportunities that we have the option of taking up or not, and most of all that means being true to ourselves. *Not me* is the kind of denial that never allows a person to hold their head up with pride about something they have done or been.

More dangerously *not me* is the kind of game that gets caught up with many other *me* diseases like *but* and a frequent denial that the negative *me* states are never my fault. Taking responsibility for your life and the lives of those around you will empower you and everyone you come in contact with. Replacing *not me* with *I can take responsibility* changes the lives of people who believed that they have suffered, will suffer and are too afraid to take a leap of faith.

I AM TAKING RESPONSIBILITY FOR MY LIFE
I AM TAKING RESPONSIBILITY TO TREAT OTHERS FAIRLY
I AM TAKING RESPONSIBILITY FOR CREATING THE ENVIRONMENT I LIVE IN

The *Carrying the World on My Shoulders* Disease

There is not a person in the world who, at some time in their life, has not been acting this one out. Particularly when we were children and had been disappointed there would have been at least a few times when we would have jumped into play-acting the part. It is, in many ways, the inverse of the *not me* disease when a person seems to take the cares of the whole world upon their shoulders and is stooping under the weight.

You can see sufferers of this disease in mental institutions as they shuffle along the corridors doing *carrying the world on my shoulders*. In order for this disease to work it requires a large physical element that sends a person into very bad posture with a collapsed back and misaligned shoulders. The eyes need to have a sad, dog-like quality while expressing a *Don't hurt me any more* look on the face. People in this mode assume a childlike position to everyone else and wear a large invisible sign stuck on their forehead which says *Victim – kick me.*

People playing this game are also very prone to addictive behaviours that include anorexia, bulimia, and substance abuse. They feel the world becomes too much for them to cope with and they choose the escapism that comes with addictive rituals and being spaced out, away from reality.

There is also an element of *not me* here because it is an abdication of responsibility of the person to defend themselves against other people dumping on them. They have convinced themselves that they have no control over their lives and procrastinate about how they are to blame for everything.

No one else is required to take part in this game because the person can play it all by themselves, although they do enjoy it when someone supports their masochism by playing a dominant role. This disease is a sign of immaturity and there are some people who never grow up but just grow older.

Since so many of our mental processes are tied up with our physiology, you will get the best results for help in overcoming the *carrying the world on my shoulders* disease by closely studying the sections on exercise and breathing. Remember, physical and mental performance are inextricably linked.

I accept responsibility for my life...and I expect others to accept responsibility for their lives too...***I CHANGE THINGS TO MAKE MY LIFE BETTER***...I can stand tall and proud as a natural right...I can help others choose to be engaged with life...***AND THE CARES I DON'T NEED TO DEAL WITH CAN FLOAT AWAY IN A BALLOON***.

The *I Can't* Disease

This is probably the most damaging of all the *me* diseases as it undermines the whole personality, limiting a person's potential to be well physically, mentally and spiritually. Furthermore the *I can't* disease installs limitations that prohibit a person from ever going onto levels of excellence in their life.

The *I can't* disease, when it is threatened, adopts a strategy of camouflage and can turn into *I won't, I don't want to, and I don't care anyway.* The subterfuge it invents to defend itself can be very creative.

Our human potential is profound, but during our lives most of us only ever scratch the surface by operating the kind of inhibitory beliefs that have been installed in us by parents, teachers, governments and even our friends. This is often done without our conscious knowledge when a series of comments or ideas have been drip-fed into our unconscious, and the conscious mind has not recognised them as being contrary to our well being.

Many people do not mean to tell us that we cannot do this or that and they are often unaware of the profound effects that derogatory comments can have on the mind's ability to block actions as well as promote potential. There are some people and institutional structures, however, that purposefully install limiting beliefs in people, either to suit themselves, that institution or society at large.

We introject (receive into our minds and self-programme) much of what is going on around us from the very early times when we are a foetus in the womb. A mother's attitude towards the baby she is carrying is so influential it can even increase or decrease the size of the foetus. A child that has had calming, relaxing music played to it during the pregnancy is much more likely to sleep well and be even tempered after it is born than a child that has been exposed to loud rock music or domestic unhappiness.

Schools indoctrinate the majority of children into believing that their potential is limited by downgrading them as being less than exceptional. The school system calls this child management and says that it is trying to match the individual child to their potential. The bare facts are, though, that it is making excuses for having too many pupils, too few teachers, and poor teaching attitudes towards and knowledge about how to teach. Those children, of course, grow up to be adults that carry around the same kind of concepts in their minds about being downgraded with limited potential.

Our social structures are always based on class systems of one kind or another, whether it be accent, wealth, education or self-efficacy (belief in the self). People who have belief in themselves are far more likely to progress in life, stay well, recover from illness, and become happy and fulfilled. Although we all have some limitations due to the length of our legs, capacity of our lungs, or height, and so on, beyond that our potential to become more than our present selves is profound.

The cure for the *I can't* disease is as simple as to change your thoughts and statements to *I can,* within realistic consideration of your circumstances. While miracles take a little longer, self-excellence is immediately available to everyone. You can constantly reprogramme your mind by putting the kinds of images and messages into your unconscious that you wish to be thinking. And remember, thoughts lead to action, so consider one of my favourite of all maxims:

IF I THINK I CAN...IF I THINK I CAN'T...I'M RIGHT EITHER WAY

At this point I shall again throw down a challenge to you. If you do not want excellence in your life, please stop reading and give this work away to someone who does. If you think you might like excellence in your life, but are too afraid you will fail, then go back to the beginning of this chapter and read it again and again until you are ready to move on.

You see, in England we have a saying which states *the proof of the pudding is in the eating.* Well...I'm eating...and I can tell you I'm eating well. In other words I personally have found excellence in my life, and in my practice helped thousands of people to do the same. The methods in this book, if you apply them rigorously, can help you, but remember this is definitely not a work to be flicked through and hope for the best. It is a blueprint for a life philosophy as well as self-hypnosis.

No one is born with *me* diseases, nor do they purposefully install those thought patterns and reactions. Some people are born with certain physical and mental differences that prevent them from participating in life in the same way as the average person, such as Downs Syndrome or autism. On the whole, however, we are all capable of excellence beyond any of our previous expectations.

The *Blinkers* Disease

Have you ever seen a horse drawing a carriage with blinkers across its eyes? Why do you think that the carriage driver has done that? Well it's simple – the carriage driver does not want the horse to have any distractions and to follow only the way ahead. Since the way ahead is the only way the horse can see, it naturally follows that road.

I can take the scales from my eyes...opening my ears to hear well...

AND BE AWARE IN EACH OF MY SENSES

Due to early childhood programming, individuals can also develop programmes that lead them to operate in one modality (one of the five senses) more than the others. For instance some people receive and give out communications better through visual cues, others manoeuvre the world by sound, and some people feel their way through life. In rarer cases some people interact with their environment through smell and taste. Different people have developed different ways of communicating that can sometimes disable and give them *blinkers* in one or more of the those senses.

I CAN ANALYSE OTHER PEOPLE'S COMMUNICATION STYLES
TAKING TIME TO HELP THEM UNDERSTAND MY COMMUNICATIONS
I AM ENJOYING BEING A PROGRESSIVE STUDENT OF
COMMUNICATION

There are people who are intensely single-minded and are focusing so hard on a narrow range of goals that they become virtually blind, deaf and unaware of the world around them. They may either be running away from something they fear or charging towards a single identified target. These people can often be very successful in business or in their own particular professional fields but they seem to have little idea what is happening with other people or the rest of the world.

"OH MY EARS AND WHISKERS, HOW LATE IT'S GETTING"
(THE WHITE RABBIT: ALICE'S ADVENTURES IN WONDERLAND)

Do you remember the White Rabbit who was so busy rushing to get somewhere and was never really fully aware of what was happening around him? The world is full of people trying to do exactly the same.

Blinkers disease is like any other *me* disease – a behaviour that is operated automatically out of conscious awareness under the control of unconscious routines. The person is often not aware that the *me* disease is happening until someone points it out or if they are aware, they do not know how to change things. If they are aware they may be too frightened to tackle the problem so they allow the *me* disease to run on uninterrupted.

As I said earlier a *me* disease can take many forms and is not restricted to the ones we have looked at in this chapter. They are compulsive behavioural loops which go on running the same old negative programmes that distract from the excellence of life. Not only are they destructive but they also prevent people getting well from illness or comfortably accepting their life as it is in the present.

Many years, sometimes a whole lifetime, can pass without a person becoming aware of the devastating effects that a *me* disease has had on their life. Sometimes people wake up at 70 or 80 years of age, having been in a trance their whole life, doing the same old *me* diseases again and again and again.

Remember, the mind is like the digestive system – what you put in governs what you become. Should you put in rubbish or poisons, the mind, body and spirit will react exactly as if you had eaten arsenic. If you put in good constructive imprinting and re-imprinting, the probability of good health, self-worth and happiness is at its highest.

Following is a general script for eradicating *me* diseases that you can use, as usual, by taping it in the middle of a trance script or learning it by heart. After you have practised it several times, you can change it, if you need to, by adding suggestions for specific changes that you think are appropriate to you, remembering to state changes in the **POSITIVE ACTIVE**.

Installing the Positive Active (Script)

I can spend this time examining my thoughts...this will be a time of self development...***I CAN RECOGNISE THE DIFFERENCE BETWEEN ACTIVE AND REACTIVE MODES***...being aware of the difference will help me be able to choose...taking control of my life at a conscious and unconscious level...***I AM ABLE TO REPROGRAMME MY MIND WHEN I NEED TO***...surveying my thoughts should I recognise a *me* disease I can change...I continually develop the ability to choose...***BECOMING POSITIVE ACTIVE THROUGH A PROCESS OF CHOICE***...whatever has happened has happened and I can accept that...taking lessons from the knowledge that is my history...***LIFE IS WHAT I DO I WITH WHAT HAS HAPPENED***...I have had many successes in my life...many of which I can review....***AND I CAN BUILD ON MY SUCCESSES TIME AND TIME AGAIN***...sometimes everyone repeats their mistakes...I can recognise when I am doing that...***IF WHAT I'M DOING IS NOT WORKING I CAN DO SOMETHING DIFFERENT***...whatever has happened to me I can learn from...whatever is happening to me at this time I can learn from...***I CAN IMPROVE MY LIFE BY THE KNOWLEDGE I HAVE GAINED***...I accept my life course...I can develop more power over the choices I can make...***I GAIN CONTROL IN THE FUTURE AND PRESENT***...no one can live my life for me...the formula for change I can recognise as being simple...**I AM TAKING RESPONSIBILITY FOR MY LIFE**...I can also treat others with consideration...my interactions with others can be caring...**I AM TAKING RESPONSIBILITY TO TREAT OTHERS FAIRLY**...as I use the earth's resources I can recognise that they are not inexhaustible...the social atmosphere I live in is partly of my making...**I CAN TAKE RESPONSIBILITY FOR CREATING THE ENVIRONMENT IN WHICH I LIVE**...I accept responsibility for my life...and I expect others to accept responsibility for their lives too...***I CHANGE THINGS TO MAKE MY LIFE BETTER***...I can stand tall and proud as a natural right...I can help others choose to be engaged with life...***AND THE CARES I DON'T NEED TO DEAL WITH CAN FLOAT AWAY IN A BALLOON***...I have the resources to live my life in a good way...finding a way that is right for me...***IF I THINK I CAN***...***IF I THINK I CAN'T***...***I'M RIGHT EITHER WAY***...communicating effectively can open many doors for me...I will constantly re-evaluate my performance...***I CAN ENJOY BEING AN EFFECTIVE COMMUNICATOR***...I can take the scales from my eyes...opening my ears to listen...**AND BE AWARE IN EACH OF MY SENSES**...I can try to understand the way other people communicate ...take the time to help them understand my communication...***I AM ENJOYING BEING A PROGRESSIVE STUDENT OF COMMUNICATION***...learning to understand myself is an honourable journey...learning to change what I can empowers me...***I AM EMPOWERED BY MY JOURNEY***...I am becoming more aware that I change in positive ways...becoming aware I can devise my own journey...***I HAVE THE POWER AND THE FREEDOM TO CHOOSE HOW MY OWN MIND WORKS***.

Summary

■ Checking for signs of the most common *me* diseases in yourself by paying attention to and analysing your thoughts, language and actions.

■ Understanding the effects that the *me* diseases have on behaviour and levels of happiness.

■ Devising trance scripts to eradicate your own negative thought and language patterns and install new, positive constructive ways of thinking and speaking.

■ Realising that it is not always necessary to understand the roots of negative patterns before they are changed into positive constructive mindsets.

■ Do the exercise on p160.

Frequently Asked Questions

Q. What if I cannot change?
A. Keep reading this chapter over and over again until you have the answer to your own question.

Q. I have been the way I was for so many years, maybe I am too old to change.
A. If you are still breathing then you are able to change. Change is inevitable in all of us and you can choose to either take control of that change or not.

Q. How do I detect the me *diseases if I am not consciously aware of them?*
A. Ask a friend to read this section and then to help you identify any me diseases or negative language patterns that they see in you. Cross-check the results with another friend separately and independently.

Q. If I have had a life of depression and I now recognise that I have been operating many me *diseases, is it possible for me to change and be normal?*
A. I hope you will never be normal, but it is possible for you to be special and

exceptional. Working on yourself daily with the self-hypnosis techniques in this book will open many possibilities up to you that perhaps you may only have ever dreamed about. Everyone is capable of creating happiness.

Further Reading

BANDLER, RICHARD & GRINDER, JOHN, **THE STRUCTURE OF MAGIC**, SCIENCE AND BEHAVIOR BOOKS, CA, USA, 1975.

BANDLER, RICHARD & GRINDER, JOHN, **THE STRUCTURE OF MAGIC II**, SCIENCE AND BEHAVIOR BOOKS, CA, USA, 1976.

BERNE, ERIC, MD, **GAMES PEOPLE PLAY**, PENGUIN BOOKS, LONDON, 1964.

CANFIELD, JACK & HANSEN, VICTOR, **A SECOND HELPING OF CHICKEN SOUP FOR THE SOUL**, HEALTH COMMUNICATIONS, FLORIDA, USA, 1995.

STETTBACHER, J KONRAD, **MAKING SENSE OF SUFFERING: THE HEALING CONFRONTATION WITH YOUR OWN PAST**, MERIDIAN GROUP, NEW YORK, 1993.

Chapter Eight

Accessing and Installing Foundation States of Being

As always in this book I have spoken to you about starting from the inside to portray outwards what you need, want or desire to experience. It is now an indisputable fact of science that all the pills in the world cannot give a person a sense of well being if they are in a poor state of mind. The religion of modern medicine has its limits; for thousands of years shamans, religious leaders, gurus, traditional medicine people, magicians and scholars have all understood how to change a person's state of being from the inside outwards.

First of all let us talk about the difference between being and doing because they really are quite different. Doing is an activity that is the pursuit of a goal and is a continual action. Doing is the action that requires perpetual effort and motion. People who are engaged in constant doing can become very tired, stressed, strung out, annoyed and bad tempered because they take little time out to enjoy the simple pleasure in life of being alive. They may be great achievers but they can find little peace and are mostly running towards something or away from something else.

Doers make great politicians, business people, and are the people who think they make the world go round. Eventually many of them can become ill with various degenerative diseases because they have failed to focus on themselves enough and have neglected their physical, mental and spiritual health.

Being is the space in time you take to pay attention to your own needs. It can be when you metaphorically stop time to analyse your perspective on life and the life you are experiencing, simply a moment of contemplation. This is a time when you cease the relentless pursuit of action and find yourself just sensing being alive. It is the state that is largely missing in the world today, which is why capitalism and consumerism are so successful because everyone is trying to buy a state of being and advertisers are trying to sell them products that promise that perfect state of being.

What most people have not been taught today is that being is not something you can buy but something you create for yourself from the inside outwards. In the East, which has been less contaminated by the ever faster moving pace of consumerism, many of the yogis and gurus still have the skill to be able to teach people about being. In the West the creation of many of those states has been forgotten, even by religions who today mainly trade in piety and dogma that has long since lost its meaning in the mouths of those who recite it parrot-like, word for word.

I CAN RECOGNISE THE DIFFERENCE BETWEEN DOING AND BEING

A balanced human being will be able to move from doing to being with ease whenever they need or want, allowing the body to rest and their mind to become detached from physical actions as they contemplate life or just experience being in existence. What the most powerful thing you can learn now is that all doing needs to start with a clear, strong, and ever powerful foundation state of being. When you do this you will find that you can do absolutely anything you want in life within your capabilities and that your capabilities are far more than you were ever consciously aware.

I ACCEPT THAT I CREATE MY OWN SENSE OF BEING FROM THE INSIDE OUTWARDS

If you look at old film footage of Gandhi, Mother Teresa, and the priests from the Shaolin temple, you will find that they all appear to have found some kind of inner strength that helps them to experience peace. This is because they all learnt to start their actions based on a foundation state they created for themselves.

People can learn the skill that the priests of the Shaolin temple are taught from the very early training that they receive. Yogis learnt to create these foundation states to have control over mind, body and spirit.

MY UNCONSCIOUS MIND HAS MILLIONS OF YEARS OF KNOWLEDGE

Hypnotists have also helped people to attain these states in the work they have done for thousands of years when they were priests in Egyptian sleep temples, healers in Greek dream temples, and Mesmers practising animal magnetism in the 18th and 19th century. Today modern hypnotists can also teach people to attain these inner states of being very quickly as you are going to learn here. You are capable of attaining these foundation states that you can start all of your doings from so that you can perform your own sense of excellence in whatever you do.

Earlier you did the...**NOW**...exercise that helped you come into the present and just experience being alive and the fact that you were alive was proof that you had evidence of success unconsciously. Many people are unsure when they begin the foundation state exercises if they can attain the states that priests or monks spend decades learning, but through hypnosis you can, and in a very short time too.

The State of Eternal Love
So many people in this world are looking desperately for other people to love them so that they can feel good. Those people never find the love they seek because the first person who needs to love you in the life equation is who...?

Many people scoff and laugh when therapists begin to talk about love and then go away privately to live their lives unhappily. Their cynicism is a defence reaction to the fear of being hurt by failing to achieve a state of love that they so desperately need, want or desire. In life it is wise to seize opportunities when they come your way just as you are doing...***NOW!***

If you were stranded on a desert island alone for the rest of your life, never to see another person, you would need to create enough love to last your whole life through. How could you do that...?

The Foundation State of Love (Script)

I can take a deep breath all the way inside myself...holding it...letting all my negative energies and thoughts become part of that outwards breath...***I CAN LET ALL MY NEGATIVE ENERGIES FLOAT OUT AND AWAY ON THAT OUT BREATH NOW!***...I search deep inside myself to find a wellspring from which flows the state of love...as I search for it I create it as an eternal ever flowing spring...***I CAN EXPERIENCE LOVE FLOWING FROM THAT SPRING NOW!***...it is not necessary for my conscious mind to understand everything that is happening...simply allowing myself to experience these good feelings ...***I CAN ALLOW THE LOVE TO FLOW OUTWARDS***...giving it colour...feeling ...texture...sound...smell and even taste...allowing it to take a form that is right for me...***I CAN LET THAT SENSE OF LOVE FLOW ETERNAL***...when I am asleep or unconscious the love will continue to flow...***I AM FILLING EVERY PART OF MY BODY...MIND...AND SOUL WITH THAT EVER FLOW-ING LOVE***...it's OK to adjust it to suit me...filling the room or space around me with that love...***I CAN ALLOW THE LOVE...MYSELF...AND THE WORLD TO EXIST IN SYMBIOSIS***...filling the town or province with that love...it still continues to flow endlessly...I allow...create...and distribute that love from the wellspring inside me...***THE MAGICIAN WITHIN ME CONTINUES TO POUR OUT THAT FLOW OF LOVE***...filling the country and continent around me...this becoming part of my automatic processes...***I AM FILLING THE WORLD...UNIVERSE...AND BEYOND WITH THE LOVE CREATED FROM WITHIN ME***...being aware that I have all the love I will ever need for myself...and that love I receive from others will be an extra bonus...***I CAN BE POWERFUL ENOUGH TO GIVE LOVE AWAY UNRESERVEDLY***...the most powerful thing in my life is to be able to do that without even telling the recipient that I am giving it to them...***I AM CREATING THE POWER FOUNDATION STATE OF ETERNAL LOVE THAT WILL CONTINUE TO FLOW AUTOMATICALLY NOW!***

When you immerse yourself in trance and create the foundation state expe-riences, do not be surprised if you begin to feel euphoric and light-headed both in and coming out of trance. The first time people experience the foun-dation state of love in trance they may even find they have tears running down their face with absolute relief and joy that they have found, for the very first time, the level of love they have sought the whole of their lives. Remember to bring those foundation states back with you out of trance to your waking life.

I CAN RE-EXPERIENCE THOSE GOOD FEELINGS EACH TIME I OPEN MY EYES

Peace

Peace, like love, means many different things to many different people. Peace comes from the action of the creation of peace as opposed to being a pre-existing entity, so we are each responsible for creating the peace we seek. The conundrum of whether the being or doing of peace comes first becomes irrelevant as you learn to create it for yourself.

The Foundation State of Peace (Script)

Just for some time I can allow the outside world to disappear...being totally inside myself alone...***I CAN FOCUS ON A COLOUR I CHOOSE TO REPRESENT PEACE TO ME***...seeing the colour building in strength...or maybe there is a representation of peace in my other senses...***I CAN BECOME MORE AWARE OF MY OWN PEACE EXPERIENCE***...allowing the sense of peace to grow in its characteristics...feeding it with my good intentions...***I TRANSPORT MYSELF TO A PLACE OF ABSOLUTE PEACE***...the world can carry on without me for a while...focusing on a sense of peace within...***I CAN INSTALL THAT PEACE INTO EACH PART OF MY BODY***...taking all the time I need inside my head...while in real time this can happen very quickly...***JUST LIKE LOVE PEACE CAN GIVE ME A SENSE OF CALMNESS AND MY OWN STRENGTH***...in a short while when I count to three I can allow that peace to double...then like a recurring multiplication it can continue to double as it fills my life...on the count of ***ONE...TWO...THREE!***

Wellness and Healing

People do not always make their own illness, but a lot of the time they are responsible for their own wellness and healing. With the assistance of good living, well being is, to a great extent, a state of mind. Shamans and medicine people in all cultures have known and used this for tens of thousands of years.

If we look at the placebo effect we can see that people who believe in their ability to get better produce more effective healing results. In today's world we have become brainwashed by the procedures that can be carried out by modern medicine and many people have forgotten about their own ability to heal themselves.

The Foundation State of Wellness and Healing (Script)

It is OK to accept that for millions of years the human body has developed healing systems...those have taken millions of years to develop effectively...***I ACCEPT MY MILLIONS OF YEARS OF GENETIC HEALING ABILITY***... perhaps it is not possible to understand all that at a conscious level...but at an unconscious level my mind and body know all about healing me...***I AM THE MOST IMPORTANT HEALER THAT I WILL EVER EXPERIENCE IN MY LIFE***...my white blood cells have many different immune functions...part of those are built-in protection against disease and invasion...***I CAN VISUALISE THOSE WHITE BLOOD CELLS PERMANENTLY PATROLLING AND GUARDING MY BODY***...they know the difference between me and foreign unwelcome bodies...any hostile alien invasions inside me can be shown the way out of my body...***I CAN ELIMINATE UNWANTED FOREIGN INVASIONS***...there is an adaptive part of my immune system that can recognise previously unrecognisable unwanted foreign bodies...this part can deal with the rest of the unwanted invading material in my body...***I CAN SEE THE ACTIONS IN MY MIND OF THE PROTECTIVE GUARDS AND GUIDES INSIDE ME THAT HELP MY BODY KEEP WELL***...my mind is a canvas on which I can draw what I need...want...or desire...my body has the ability to improve my immune system anytime it needs...***I AM THE MAGICIAN HEALER INSIDE MYSELF***...my body's ability to flood me with oxygen can also fuel that process...any healing mechanism I do not understand consciously will work naturally automatically unconsciously...***I HELP AND TRUST MY UNCONSCIOUS TO DO ITS VERY BEST FOR ME***...up ahead in the distance I can see a bright healing light...my unconscious can recognise the power of the light...***I CAN ALLOW THE LIGHT TO COME TOWARDS ME WITH ITS HEALING POWER***...I know I do not have to understand everything consciously...as the light comes to me it is possible to walk into the light...***I ALLOW MYSELF TO BATHE IN THE HEALING LIGHT***...its power comes into me...surrounds me...breathing it in as it fills me...the time has come for the light and I to join as one...being in harmony...***I AM THE HEALING LIGHT***.

State of Oneness

One of the most important themes that I have spoken about is the development of the self as we learn and relearn to live in harmony with ourselves, other people, creatures and the environment. This is a journey I have had to travel myself, learning to develop my philosophy for life in accordance with the things others have taught me along the way.

Although I was brought up with a mother who was Church of England, a father who was Catholic, ancestors who were Jewish and Pagan, my own journey has led me to become a humanist. I deplore prejudice and bigotry of any kind and have spent a great deal of my life campaigning for fair treatment of all and propose to do so until my last dying breath.

I believe humanity has gone too far in its exploitation of the earth's resources and destroying the ecology of the planet. We are exploiting animals for food and clothing, and are doing nothing less than torturing them in laboratories in the misguided name of science. Since I was brought up in the country as a meat eating, leather and fur wearing beneficiary of medical procedures carried out on animals, my own personal journey has been a very long one.

As I write this I have been a vegetarian on and off for 30 years but have only been a vegan for three years and it has taken a long time to eventually eradicate all the traces of dead animals from my home and life. Becoming a raw food vegan has taken me to a place of personal and social enlightenment that I had not dreamed possible when I was younger and I am healthier, happier and spiritually wealthier than I have ever been.

For every person's conversion to vegetarianism the food chain would feed at least six more people in the third world. More livestock do not add to the amount of food available for people: on the contrary, they compete for resources. It takes approximately 4kg of grain to produce 1kg of pork and 3kg to produce every kg of eggs[1].

Animal farming is not effective – it takes up too much space per mouthful and destroys many of the natural ecological characteristics of the land. There is no kind way to kill an animal for food, clothing or other products and it is time we began as a species to wake up to the havoc and cruelty we are wreaking on the planet we live on and the lives of the creatures we share it with.

I share with you the fact that I am a vegan, non-animal product wearing or using, non-racist, non-sexist, recycling, socialist, humanitarian, egalitarian ecologist because that is my pleasure. It took me a long time to get here and *I can tell you* this is a good place to be which will help to guarantee me and those that come after me the ability to enjoy the fruits of nature, not just leaving spoils. **Remember**...**and remember very well**...the world is ruled by politicians, not wise people so it is up to wise people to leave politicians in no doubt about what is wise.

Installing and exploring the sense of oneness is a very spiritual experience, even for those of us who have a non-denominational sense of god, whatever that is to each and every individual.

The Foundation State of Oneness (Script)

There is a part of my life that is exclusively for my own needs...beyond that sharing much of existence with everyone and everything else can be a pleasure...***I CAN LEARN TO BE AT ONE WITH THE WORLD***...thinking what exactly does such a statement mean to me...is it an expression of mutual respect for the rest of existence and expecting the same for myself...***I CAN HAVE A CONTINUAL JOURNEY OF DISCOVERY***...what is it I do in my daily life that shows such respect...powerfully I can initiate the question and equation perpetuating the cycle...***I CAN REACH OUT MY HAND AND MIND TO THE REST OF EXISTENCE AND CONNECT POSITIVELY***...some of the connections I get back will receive information including distress...the analysing of that material can allow me to continually change the ways I connect with the rest of the world...***I AM A CREATOR OF THE ONENESS AND A RECIPIENT OF IT TOO***...treating animals with the respect that enriches their lives...being aware that plant life is living and sustains us...***I CAN RE-ASSESS THE WAYS I REACT TO NATURE***...being at one with the world can allow me to be at one with myself as I experience many good things...spending time just to enjoy those benefits...***I CAN ENJOY BEING CONNECTED WITH EVERYTHING POSSIBLE AS ONE***...sometimes that does not require words or thoughts but is simply an unconscious aware-ness...it can always be part of my underlying life philosophy as I think about and plan my actions...***I CAN FEEL THE CONNECTIONS BUILDING AS I AM BEING AT ONE WITH LIFE IN THE WAY I LIVE***.

Personal Excellence

We can all have a sense of being that is our personal excellence, no matter what the life course we take or the circumstances in which we live. Most peo-ple are, however, unaware that such a state exists. Such people would also have great difficulties believing you if you told them that such a state exists because their belief systems perpetuate the myth that they are limited by their own inadequacies. If you are one of these people, go to the section on beliefs and install the belief that you can attain your own sense of excellence.

HEAVEN IS WHAT I CAN BECOME

I do not mean here that you should be perfect all, or even part, of the time, but that your existence is underpinned by the fundamental beliefs and feel-ings that you can be the very best that is possible for you. Even having attained your sense of excellence I would not want you to never err again because that would be unrealistic and not at all human. It does not matter what you do, where you live, or who you are, the foundation state of excellence can be available to you, and it is not measured by judgementalism.

The Foundation State of Personal Excellence (Script)

It is possible to remember the ***NOW!*** exercise I did...the fact that I live and breathe means that I am a success...***I CAN BE AWARE THAT I HAVE SUC-CESSES JUST BY BEING***...from each experience in life it is possible to learn...constructive information that others give to me and I gather myself can help me to adjust as well...***I CAN ACCEPT AND UNDERSTAND THAT ALL INFORMATION GIVES ME FEEDBACK ABOUT MY ACTIONS AND MY***

STATES OF BEING...nothing I do will make me less human than anyone else...everything I do can be a construction of an action due to my present level of knowledge...**I CAN CONSTANTLY ADD TO MY KNOWLEDGE ABOUT EVERYTHING**...nothing in the world will ever cause me to give up in my quest for personal excellence...every day I can reinvent myself anew...**RESTING HERE IN TRANCE MY EXISTENCE CAN EXPAND BEYOND MY PHYSICAL SELF**...it is possible to expand my sense of being to accomplish personal excellence in any area of my life...the act of doing this in my mind can give me a great sense of worth...**I**...**MY BEING**...**MY ACTIONS**...**AND THE SENSE OF EXCELLENCE BECOME ONE**...I do not have to understand all things consciously as excellence is an experience...throughout my life in the future things will seem different...enthusiasm can build about my abilities to perform...**I CAN BECOME MY FOUNDATION STATE OF EXCELLENCE** ...each day this can be reinstalled at an unconscious and conscious level...continually repeating the statement that my abilities can attain excellence...**EACH DAY THE SUN CAN RISE INSIDE MY HEAD BEFORE I OPEN MY EYES AND GET OUT OF BED**...despite all the obstacles that impede anyone in life I can find ways to go forward positively...nothing can deter me from my quest to be my own personal best...**AS I WAKE UP I WILL EXPERIENCE THE FOUNDATION STATE OF EXCELLENCE BEING PART OF ME**...**IN EVERYTHING I DO**.

Happiness and Laughter

So many people come to see me complaining about unhappiness, depression, hopelessness and despair. Many of them have often been through the psychiatric system and have had varying assortments of pills prescribed to them that have rarely solved their problems in the long run.

Here I will tell you that the only way to long-term happiness in your life is through thinking and changing your thoughts and ideas if they are not working for you – *no one else is going to do it for you.*

A good therapist will help you do that and they will teach you what you can do to change your life but, at the end of the day, if you do not do the work inside your head regularly the results will not happen by themselves.

Each day of my life I work with myself in the trance state, maintaining my well being and installing new programmes in my mind that can help me conquer new tasks. Since I truly had a great deal of unhappiness in my early life I know full well that if I want to keep myself in a good frame of mind then I need to be my own caretaker inside my head.

One of my favourite comedians of all time is the Englishman Ken Dodd, who as part of his repertoire, referred to his chuckle muscle and the fact that not only did it need to be exercised regularly but also tickled. Have you tickled your chuckle muscle today?

The Happiness and Laughter Button (Script)

It is easy for anyone to conceive that the mind...body...and spirit are connected...our moods are initiators of and responses to life...***I CAN CHANGE MY MOOD BY CHANGING MY MIND***...inside my mind I can see a large bright button up ahead...written on it are the capital letters **L** and **H** in good colours...***IN MY MIND I CAN CONNECT THIS BUTTON TO MY STATE OF MIND...BODY...AND SPIRIT***...the **L** is for laughter that needs no reason to happen...**H** is for the happy hormones that circulate my body doing their job...***EACH TIME I SEE THE FACES OF THE HAPPINESS HORMONES IT CAN MAKE ME SMILE***...recalling the many funny experiences in my life I can re-experience those good feelings again...laughter I know is so good for me...***WHEN I PUSH THE L AND H BUTTON I WILL EXPERIENCE LAUGHTER AND HAPPINESS HORMONES***...this does not have to show externally every time...however there will always be a bodily expression...***I AM BECOMING IN CONTROL OF MY OWN GOOD MOODS NATURALLY***...people will notice a difference but I don't have to tell them everything...sometimes I can have a pleasant secret to myself...***I CAN ENJOY BEING ABLE TO FEEL GOOD ON CUE AS I PUSH THE L AND H BUTTON IN MY OWN MIND NOW!***...it is good to know I can do this whenever I want...prescribing as much good feeling to myself as I need...want...or...desire...***I CAN PRESS IT AGAIN NOW!...AND AGAIN...AND AGAIN...AND AGAIN!***

The Third Eye

As this work is as much about life philosophy as it is about self-hypnosis, I wanted to share with you one of the most important experiences of my life that I underwent in Australia. During my stay there I spent time in the Sydney museums learning about the aboriginal culture and how it had been almost wiped out by more than 200 years of invasion by other races.

As I sat talking to an Aboriginal man he explained to me that even until the beginning of the 1980s their children were being kidnapped by white missionaries and brought up as non-Aborigines. This left generations of teenagers going out into the world as Aborigines without any knowledge of their own culture. He also talked about how the invading Europeans and later Asians had devastated the natural ecological state of the land so that in many ways it no longer resembled the continent it had been for thousands of years. This he described as the foreigners' disease of blindness for the balance of nature.

We cannot go on destroying the planet we live on in the way we have. Since the beginning of the industrial revolution we have been devastating and disturbing our environment – what the Gaia theory determines as the slow death of a living planet. We are all part of the earth's ecology and at this moment in time not a very clever part.

The old Aboriginal man told me that as soon as a lost teenage Aborigine turns up looking for their roots he takes them out into the bush to undergo a ceremony for getting back in touch with nature. A third eye is painted on their forehead with ochre which is a metaphorical and spiritual reconnection to the way they can see their lives and their interaction with the living land and nature. The Aborigines know their way around the bush, across a desert and about the land because they are able to use their third eye.

The social psychologist Piaget talked about the different stages that human beings pass through as they grow up. First they can only see the world from their own perspective and after a while they learn to see things from someone else's view as well. Maturity, however, only occurs when they are able to see themselves and their actions from several points of view and are able to alter their actions according to the effectiveness of those actions on themselves, others and in the larger environment.

I CAN GROW UP AS WELL AS GROWING OLDER

The way in which you live your life depends on your ability to use your third eye to balance your interactions with yourself, people around you and the world in which you live. It is always preferable to leave the place you have visited better for you having been there.

Rediscovering the Third Eye (Script)

Life is a journey during which time my mind can grow...my body makes an impression where I have been...***I CAN CHOOSE WHAT KIND OF IMPRESSION I LEAVE ON THE WORLD***...as I go through life there can be a realisation that choices are available to me...an attitude of mind creates an attitude to life...***I CAN REDISCOVER MY THIRD EYE AS I PAINT IT ON MY FOREHEAD IN MY MIND***...using the brush of knowledge to outline that third all-seeing eye in the middle of my forehead...being aware as I paint its design in my mind that there are other views...***REACTING TO THE WORLD AND LIFE BY SEEING A GREATER AND BIGGER PICTURE***...it will further give me a clear view of how I can operate within myself...me watching me in the world and feeding back that information...***AND AT THE END OF EACH DAY I CAN APPRECIATE THAT LIFE IS NOT ALWAYS JUST ABOUT ME***...my relationship with life can become like the Aborigines' relationship with the land...respecting it...revering it...using it...but not abusing it...***MY ABILITY TO SEE DIFFERENTLY FEELS EXCITING AND MEANINGFUL***...this can give me different perspectives on my actions...abilities to consider the path to be taken in the future...***MY THIRD EYE CAN HELP ME LIVE MY LIFE ENJOYABLY AND MEANINGFULLY***...the third eye also connects me to my spiritual experience of being alive in a world that is alive...knowing that the spirits of my forebears and decendants will be proud of me for connecting to my third eye...***AS I LEARN MORE ABOUT MY SPIRITUAL LIFE I CAN PASS THOSE GOOD EXPERIENCES TO OTHERS KINDLY***.

Summary
■ Differentiating and recognising the difference between doing and being. Appreciating the qualities and necessity for each mode of existence.

■ Identifying the different internal foundation states of being and learning to create them inside yourself, working outwards.

■ Starting each action in your life with a foundation state that can underpin the effectiveness and integrity of your behaviour.

■ Cueing your laughter and happiness button, then installing it at the end of each of your daily trances. Learning to press it whenever you want to change and enhance your moods.

■ Rediscovering your third eye as you reintegrate yourself back into nature, taking care to take care of taking care.

■ Do the exercises on p171, p172, and p173.

Frequently Asked Questions
Q. It feels weird getting into all this love, peace and healing, and I'm sure my friends are going to think I've gone soft, so can I keep it all to myself?

A. Friends love you no matter what you are and if they do not then they are not truly your friends. What is the point of feeling good if you are keeping it all to yourself?

Repressing good feelings is a very damaging way to live your life as it causes physical illness, mental anxiety and detachment from your spiritual self. If you have happiness, peace, love, joy, health and any good feelings, spread them around. If you have learnt how to create those from the inside out, you will be producing endless amounts. People are attracted to positive people.

Q. I found the happiness and laughter button amazing but there are times when I am down and I forget to use it. What can I do?

A. No one should be in an up mood all of their life because that would be unnatural. Down moods have a purpose which is to alert us to the fact that change is happening or needs to happen; however, use the L and H button regularly at the end of your trances to top up your happy hormones daily. I remember the best funeral I ever went to was in New Orleans and when everybody had finished crying they had a party which went on for two whole days. It was the best party I ever went to, so whenever I remember my dead friend I burst into laughter. It's OK to be human.

Q What if all I do is give my resources of eternal love to some people and they never give me anything back?

A. Then both you and they will benefit from your state of mind and humanity. Give love because you want to give it and ask nothing in return. From time to time, use disassociation in trance to reassess the situation to see how you can go forward, moving yourself away from harm. When in doubt ask your uncon-

scious to let you know what to do for the best because there will be some peo-ple who it will not be healthy for you to be around at particular times.

Q. If I am connecting to the state of universal oneness of everyone and every-thing, then am I not also taking in all the bad stuff as well?
A. As you work through all the techniques, suggestions and hypnosis that you learnt from this work you will become a stronger, kinder, and smarter person. I have an innate belief, like the majority of humanity, good always eventually triumphs over bad. As you develop as a person, becoming your own version of goodness, you will infect everything you come into contact with, with that good-ness...Remember you are your own magician.

Reference
1. Feed the World: The Vegetarian Solution by Mark Gold, Outrage (magazine of Animal Aid), March 1999.

Further Reading

ANDREAS, CONNIRAE & ANDREAS, TAMARA, **CORE TRANSFORMATION: REACHING THE WELL SPRING WITHIN**, REAL PEOPLE PRESS, UTAH, USA, 1994.

CHOPRA, DEEPAK, MD, **QUANTUM HEALING: EXPLORING THE FRON-TIERS OF MIND/BODY MEDICINE**, BANTAM BOOKS, DOUBLEDAY DELL, NEW YORK, 1991.

HO, MAE-WAN, **GENETIC ENGINEERING: DREAM OR NIGHTMARE?**, GATEWAY, DUBLIN, IRELAND, 1998.

LOVELOCK, JAMES, **A NEW LOOK AT LIFE ON EARTH**, OXFORD UNIVER-SITY PRESS, NEW YORK, 1979.

LOVELOCK, JAMES, **THE AGES OF GAIA**, OXFORD UNIVERSITY PRESS, NEW YORK, 1988.

MASON, JIM, **AN UNNATURAL ORDER: WHY WE ARE DESTROYING THE PLANET AND EACH OTHER**, THE CONTINUUM PUBLISHING CO, NEW YORK, 1993.

MOONDANCE, WOLF, **SPIRIT MEDICINE: NATIVE AMERICAN TEACHINGS TO AWAKEN THE SPIRIT**, STERLING PUBLISHING, NEW YORK, I995.

PECK, M SCOTT, **THE ROAD LESS TRAVELLED AND BEYOND**, SIMON & SCHUSTER, NEW YORK, 1997.

ROSSI, ERNEST L, **MIND BODY THERAPY: METHODS OF IDEODYNAMIC HEALING IN HYPNOSIS**, WW NORTON & CO, NEW YORK & LONDON, 1994.

ROSSI, ERNEST L, **THE PSYCHOBIOLOGY OF MIND-BODY HEALING**, WW NORTON & CO, NEW YORK & LONDON, 1993.

SIMONTON, O CARL, MD, SIMONTON-MATTHEWS, STEPHANIE & CREIGHTON, JAMES L, **GETTING WELL AGAIN**, BANTAM BOOKS, LONDON, 1978.

SVOBODA, ROBERT E, **AYURVEDA: LIFE, HEALTH & LONGEVITY**, PENGUIN, LONDON, 1992.

Chapter Nine

Confidence Building

I get a lot of people telephoning me and asking to be helped with their low levels of confidence. What I immediately tell them is that I do not help anyone with low levels of confidence, but I do help people gain more and good levels of confidence. Just as you are thinking as you are reading this, it is, as usual, all in the structure of your internal thought processes, plus the language you use to yourself and others

One of the great mysteries of life for me has been why education teaches children maths, French, music and so on, yet I have far less frequently encountered school programmes that show students how to have confidence. Neither do educational programmes generally teach people to look after themselves. It is almost as if there is a conspiracy going on that makes people too embarrassed to talk about such subjects.

People can also have a lack of confidence because their parents have had little confidence, therefore, not having confidence is what they have passed on. As silly as this may seem, it is, in fact, what often happens within some families as the older generations pass on their negative behaviours and nuances to their offspring. It is a common fact that confident parents are more likely to produce confident children.

Due to a traumatic incident or encounter, a person's confidence can also be shattered at any time in their lives. This often happens to soldiers who were in combat, individuals who are attacked or abused, and victims of physical accidents or disease.

We have undoubtedly all, at some time in our lives, suffered from a crisis of confidence, portraying the inability to act or react appropriately to a situation. This does not mean we were any less of a person, simply that we did not have the skills we needed to handle the situation at that particular time. There is no shame involved in this scenario and I would like you to think of such a time as an opportunity to learn something new about yourself and others.

KNOWLEDGE IS POWER

There are, of course, people and groups who have an investment in others not having confidence. These include slave owners in third world countries who want their workers to be docile, parents who are sublimating the challenges from their offspring, teachers who suppress their students, employers attempting to control their workforce, politicians who prefer their critics to be silent, large corporations who lie about the effects of their products, drug companies who prefer their clients did not ask too much about side effects, religions whose propaganda has come under closer scrutiny and been seen to be flawed, and finally governments, which much of the time govern by secrecy rather than consent.

ACQUIRED CONFIDENCE ABILITY SKILLS

There is no magic that will suddenly make someone more confident, because confidence is a behaviour that grows out of the acquired ability to deal with situations in a positive and constructive manner. If a person does not do the work to learn those skills that will enable them to deal with the situation confidently, it simply will not happen.

ACTING AND NOT REACTING

Many people, however, mistake aggression for confidence and get themselves into all sorts of trouble when situations do not ultimately go according to their needs, wants or desires. Aggression causes other people to be defensive, puts their guard up, closes down communications, creates misunderstandings, and in turn they can become aggressive in response. What you need to do is become a communications and negotiation expert because it is your life and if you want it to go a certain way, no one else can make that happen but you!

I CAN BECOME AN EXPERT ON MY OWN COMMUNICATION ABILITIES

This will require the studying of how to programme and reprogramme your mind on your part. It will not happen in one or even five days but will take time for you to learn to act and not simply react as you might once have done. Taking responsibility for and control of your own communications gives you personal power in a wider range of situations. Even when it is appropriate for you to react you can be in control of those reactions,which is a better option. If you think this is very controlled and contrived, you are absolutely right.

HOW CAN I READ OTHER PEOPLE'S COMMUNICATIONS CLEARLY?

I can tell you that the many hours I have spent studying body language, facial expressions, communication styles, language patterns and content of communications has paid off a thousand fold, not only professionally, but also in my personal relationships. When clients say to me that they simply have not got the time to do that, my reply is always the same:

I CAN MAKE THE TIME TO STUDY MYSELF

In the first analysis the phrase s*elf-image* linguistically implies it is how we see our own visual image of ourselves inside our heads. Our self-image, however, also incorporates how we hear, taste, smell and feel about ourselves. All five senses are involved in the way we conceive our own lives, capabilities, potential, deficits, and sense of occupying space and time.

So How Do Our Concepts of Self-Image Arise?

Many building blocks of identity arise biologically as our physiological make-up is, to a large part, predetermined by our genetic-make up. On top of that we are then affected by our environmental circumstances, the food we eat, the air we breathe, our state of physical, mental and spiritual development and our life experiences. Have we introjected (taken into ourselves) positive, negative or neutral messages about ourselves and the way others see us?

You can put time aside to look at the effects that interpersonal relationships with parents, siblings, relatives, teachers, colleagues, neighbours and friends can have had on the forming and changing of your personality.

One of the analogies I like to use with people is that we all have a backpack of ideas that we carry through life, putting thoughts into it. Everyone we meet puts something into the backpack in or out of our conscious awareness. Sometimes we need to take stock of what is in that backpack of ideas we are carrying around with us. Is it useful information and images of ourselves that we are using to back us up, or are they negative ideas that make it seem as if we are carrying the whole world on our shoulders?

From time to time we need to have a look in the backpack and see what we want to keep and what we want to dispose of by throwing it away or giving the idea back to the person who gave it to us. Some of the material we may be carrying around with us may no longer be appropriate to our present lives and there may also be a need to put new ideas in the backpack.

Sorting out the Backpack (Script)

It is all right to consider all the thoughts that I have gathered about myself and the world...ideas that have come from many different sources...**IN MY BACKPACK OF LIFE I HAVE CARRIED MANY USEFUL IDEAS ABOUT MYSELF**...these positive ideas will have served me very well...they will have positively helped me do and be many things...**GOOD LEARNINGS AND IDEAS ADD TO MY ABILITIES AND POSITIVE SELF-IMAGE**...mother ...father...aunts...teachers...cousins...advertisers and many other sources have placed ideas about me and the world in my backpack...while many of these ideas will have been positive some will have had negative connotations ...**SORTING THROUGH THE BACKPACK I CAN LET THE NEGATIVE AND DETRIMENTAL MESSAGES AND IDEAS DETACH THEMSELVES**...these negative messages may have been useful once but no longer are...they might never have been useful but slipped past my conscious defences...*I TAKE*

RESPONSIBILITY FOR HAVING PUT MANY MESSAGES ABOUT MYSELF INTO MY OWN MIND...it's good to keep the positive constructive material that helps me see myself in good ways...helping me to lead a fun and rewarding life...***I CAN GIVE AWAY ANY NEGATIVE MESSAGES BACK TO THE ORIGINATORS METAPHORICALLY IN MY MIND***...these may even have been messages that were positive at the time but no longer are relevant...I can store the learnings I have had from those messages...***AND THROW AWAY THE IDEAS THAT ARE NO LONGER APPLICABLE TO ME***...new space appears in my backpack as it becomes lighter...what would I like ...need...or desire to fill those spaces...***I CAN CHOOSE TO PUT NEW***... ***POSITIVE***...***CONSTRUCTIVE***...***ACTIVE MESSAGES ABOUT MY ABILITIES IN THE BACKPACK***...suddenly it seems much lighter as I am more in control of the contents of my mind...I can be as creative as I like about what I put into the backpack...***I AM ENJOYING THE MESSAGES I AM GIVING TO MYSELF ABOUT MY SELF-IMAGE***...NAMING THOSE MESSAGES NOW!

Levels of Self-Esteem

One of the things that always comes up when looking at the way low achievers operate is that they often suffer from a low self-esteem. This is a consistent fact throughout all the work I do with clients that surfaces again and again. Our society insists on grading people according to other's standards but that frequently prevents many people from self-actualising (becoming the very best they can be). The grading system can turn into a vicious loop of thoughts, for example:

I am graded therefore I cannot achieve the level above my grade.
I cannot achieve the next level because I know my grade.
I am graded therefore I cannot achieve the level above my grade.
I cannot achieve the next level because I know my grade.

Breaking the loop and finding a new loop to play to yourself will help you achieve anything you want. I have found that people are always more intelligent, in every way, than they think they are. Our social structure has an interest in keeping the majority of people functioning at structured levels in order to service the dynamics of social order.

We can also consider the sociological factors involved in the forming of our personalities. No society constantly offers us positive images of ourselves and often threatens us as though we are alien or substandard. For instance, a person can receive hostility if they are a particular race, religion, profession, sex, sexuality or class. The reverse is also true as certain sectors of society can get preferential treatment.

A combination of all of these factors helps to form the images, sounds, feelings, tastes, smells and thoughts that we think represent ourselves to ourselves and to others too.

Taking Charge of Self-Image (Script)

A living organism is constantly changing and change is inevitable...change will always take place and that principle cannot be halted...***I CAN LEARN TO TAKE CHARGE OF MY OWN SELF-IMAGE***...today will become last week and last year will become a decade ago...we will change relative to time and space...***I CAN HAVE ALL THE TIME I NEED INSIDE MY HEAD TO MAKE CHANGES NOW!***...it is all right to acknowledge the only magic is the magic I make for myself...such reality testing can give me a good basis to start the changes I need to make...***I AM CONSTANTLY BUILDING CONFIDENCE***...If I know nothing then I have no skills...a journey to acquire self-image building is a thirst for knowledge...***I AM ACCEPTING THAT KNOWLEDGE IS POWER***...it is good to constantly investigate ways of learning new self-image skills...firstly being happy with who I am I can add to my personal repertoire...***ACQUIRING CONFIDENCE ABILITY SKILLS***...becoming an exquisite communicator will give me many benefits in my life...that is an undeniable fact...***I CAN BECOME AN EXPERT ON MY OWN COMMUNICATION ABILITIES***...my life is often an interaction with others...this can give me and others the ability to benefit...***I CAN LEARN TO READ OTHER PEOPLE'S COMMUNICATIONS MORE CLEARLY***.

The Untold Truth About Self-Image

The real untold truth about self-image is that there is no standard image that equals success, either in an academic concept or on a personal level. As human beings we are all quite different and none of us function or react the same. What we are often unaware of, however, is how much we pick up beliefs about success from advertisers who want to relieve us of the money in our pockets.

To disempower those who try to push us into nice tidy little boxes, numbers or labels and tell us what we can and cannot do, we need to jettison many of our old beliefs about ourselves. We receive millions of pieces of information per minute and among that information we ingest subliminal messages that have been given by others. Those pieces of information may not be applicable to our well being or can act as sabotaging viruses within our minds.

I CAN UNDERSTAND I AM RESPONSIBLE FOR MAKING MY OWN TRUTHS

Oh, and just in case you should fall into the trap of thinking that I am telling you the truth about how to be confident, I would like to tell you that there is no such thing as truth either – is there?

Taking Things to Heart

People who take things too much to heart become wounded people and are taking the events in life as a personal slight against themselves. This is a negative reactive way of operating that does not give you any benefits. While it may seem personal when someone else treats you unkindly, you can come to view such incidents as an inability on their part to behave constructively and well, and as an inability on your part to see it coming.

I CAN MOVE ON BECOMING MORE AWARE OF THE MECHANICS OF LIFE

Self-pity and pity for others is rarely constructive but what can be a good move is looking for the positive ways forwards. People who allow their hearts to rule their heads constantly get into terrible trouble when they do not carefully weigh up the consequences of their actions. People who think with their minds first can allow their hearts the luxury and protection of having a much greater sense of love and well being.

MY HEART AND MIND CAN WORK EMPATHETICALLY

Films, romantic novels and advertising in the 20th century often sold people the idea of helplessness in that someone else was going to come along to solve their problems and give them excellence. When people talk about romantic notions of following their heart – what they are forgetting to say is that a heart alone without a head is not a heart at all, because a heart is only living as long as it is attached to a thinking head.

Time Management

Time is one of the most important factors involved in people taking power over their lives because if your time is not managed properly it can destroy the very foundations of the work you are doing with yourself. People make all sorts of excuses about how they were too busy, late, pressured or somehow disadvantaged, when putting off tasks.

MY DIARY CAN BE ONE OF MY BEST FRIENDS

We have a rule in our house that if it is not in the diary do not expect anyone to turn up. Because my partner and I both have full-time careers it is essential that we plan our schedules very carefully in advance. We can often be seen working late into the night at our computers, and because I am self-employed, if I do not work I do not eat.

I CAN PLAN MY WORK…SOCIAL…AND PERSONAL DIARY

I can often find myself booked for a conference more than a year in advance and I need to let people know that I will not be available for other engagements during those periods. With our lives being so full we diary eating, spending time together, family time, friends time, study time, time for ourselves, and play time. This means that planning is absolutely essential for us and the only thing that overrides that is illness or family emergencies when we drop everything to come to the assistance of those we love.

I WILL BE AWARE THAT PERSONAL WELFARE TAKES PRIORITY IN MY LIFE AND OVERRIDES ALL OTHER COMMITMENTS

When I work with couples or families, one of the issues that often arises is that people become resentful because they think others are not paying proper attention to them. This in turn causes a crisis of confidence for the aggrieved person who thinks that perhaps they are not worth bothering with or they get angry because they think that the other person thinks they are not worth bothering with. This is often not true, but what has happened is that people have not communicated their intentions properly to others or they have got themselves in a mess because they find they do not have time left for themselves or their loved ones due to poor planning and time management.

BEWARE THE THIEF OF TIME

Putting in the Effort

People are really very pleasantly surprised how quickly they can turn around a poor self-image into feelings of confidence about themselves and their abilities. They start at the beginning of the journey wondering if it will work for them but if you put in the effort the results consistently emerge. I have a formula that...*I WANT YOU TO MEMORISE*...that will serve you very well:

EFFORT (E) + TIME (T) + TECHNIQUE (TE) = RESULTS + SELF TRADEMARK®

E + T + TE = ®

As one of my favourite teachers used to tell me as a child *IT IS NOT WHERE YOU START IT IS WHERE YOU FINISH*. Another one of her little ditties when her pupils appeared not to be putting in the effort was *YOU GET NOTHING FOR NOTHING*. My favourite saying that she used to whisper in my ear, which I never really truly understood for many years, was *ALL THE PLEASURES IN LIFE ARE OUT THERE WAITING FOR YOU TO WAKE UP AND FIND THEM*.

Arranging My Life (Script)

Whatever I want to achieve can be thought of first in my mind...constructing all the elements of that need, want or desire...*I CAN UNDERSTAND I AM*

RESPONSIBLE FOR MAKING MY OWN TRUTHS...things do not just happen to me because I am generally responsible for my life...future circumstances are made from each small step I take...*I CAN MOVE ON BECOMING MORE AWARE OF THE MECHANICS OF LIFE*...planning with my head I can provide my heart with good conditions...following my dreams in an effective and well planned way...*MY HEART AND MIND CAN WORK EMPATHETICALLY*...structuring time opportunistically can give me maximum advantages...it is easy to be adaptable when needs be...*I CAN PLAN MY WORK...SOCIAL...AND PERSONAL DIARY*...only by being strong can I help myself and others...creating a solid foundation for being me...*I WILL BE AWARE THAT PERSONAL WELFARE TAKES PRIORITY IN MY LIFE AND OVERRIDES ALL OTHER COMMITMENTS*...this is the time I can give to myself...the good effort I put into my self-image will produce benefits ...*EFFORT + TIME + TECHNIQUE = RESULTS*...I can think of the world as a place of opportunities...those opportunities are waiting for a catalyst to make them happen...*I CAN BE AWARE THAT MY MIND IS THE KEY TO MAKING MY LIFE HAPPEN AS AND WHEN I WANT IT TO HAPPEN*.

Screening

I wonder if you have ever had one of those answerphones where you can listen to the messages without picking up the receiver and taking the call. It allows you to find out who is calling and what they are saying before you decide whether you want to accept the call or not. Think about the process that is going on and install the same process in your own mind so that you screen the messages that are being given to you from the outside world.

I CAN ACCEPT POSITIVE INFORMATION AND QUESTION NEGATIVE MESSAGES

Instead of just accepting everything that is shown or told to you, set up a clearing house in your mind which screens each of the communications you receive so they can be examined and judged as to whether taking on board that information would be good for you or not. Expand time in your head each time you get a communication so you do the analysis at an unconscious level in a matter of a few seconds.

Filtering

Allow your unconscious mind to reject any messages that may be detrimental to your psyche and to alert you to the contents of those messages so that you can ignore or challenge them, even asking for clarification of the meaning. Because we receive so many pieces of information at such a phenomenal rate the conscious mind does not have the ability to monitor all of those small chunks that make up the whole. The unconscious, on the other hand, does have the ability to do that. So it is in the unconscious, during trance, that you need to install those filtering mechanisms.

IT'S ALL RIGHT TO PICK AND CHOOSE WHAT I LET INTO MY MIND

Think about it – would you like tea leaves in your tea? The bitter taste of pips in your grapes? Pieces of rock in your petrol? Most people are allowing a massive amount of unnecessary negative and destructive information to be fed into their minds when they could be installing programmes to filter it out before it becomes part of the psyche.

Looking at the Surface and Deep Structure of Communications

There is a branch of linguistics called transformational grammar, extolled by the famous linguist Noam Chomsky and later by two famous hypnotists, Richard Bandler and John Grinder. What it does is look at communications and see if the communication that is portraying the message from the communicator really reflects the meaning they meant to get across. People often do not say what they mean and somewhere along the way the communication has become corrupted so it comes out wrong. Remember earlier I asked you to stop in the middle of an action and write down the thoughts that you believed drove the action to see if they were congruent with that action?

The original message you meant to give is called the root structure and the message that really comes out is called the surface structure. When the two do not match it is said that the root structure is detached from the surface structure and the original communication is damaged. These are the communications that start and maintain wars, bad feelings, misunderstandings and give people feelings of poor self-worth and low self-esteem, because they are giving the wrong messages.

I CAN CHECK IF I AM GIVING A CLEAR COMMUNICATION (CONGRUENCY)

It is easy to take offence when other people are poor communicators and you may think they are being unkind, unhelpful or nasty. As you screen and analyse negative messages it can often become clear that the people who made those messages may have not been thinking or acting clearly. Ask yourself: *What did they really mean to communicate?*

Does their body language, voice tone, and delivery really match the content of what they are saying? Do you think they have portrayed themselves clearly?

WHAT IS THE PERSON OPPOSITE ME REALLY TRYING TO SAY?

You are not a cold person simply because you are analysing communications as they are happening but you are thinking before you implement actions or reactions and that is a good thing to do for you and others. This allows you to use your knowledge to make good judgements.

If we analyse the structure of the word *confidence* and its linguistic roots we can see that it means the bringing together of knowledge and also being in the know. Think about that as you break down confidence into manageable learnable pieces and put it all together in your behaviour.

Converting

This mechanism has four levels relying on screening, filtering, and separating out the surface structure of other people's communications and then finding their root structure by asking them more information. The conversion from the surface structure into the root structure of the communication can then give you the kind of information that can help your communication back to them be effective.

AS I ENCOUNTER COMMUNICATIONS I CAN SEARCH FOR THE ROOT MEANINGS

When you convert in this way you must always check back with the originator of the communication that your clarification is what they really meant to say. It is very important to do this because if you do not you may be in danger of projecting your imagined meaning onto their communication wrongly.

Generally people are not aware that their surface communication has become detached from their root communication and they try to defend the surface communication as being the true one. They can move into defensive mode, being entrenched in their surface communication so you need to be very disassociated, clear and unchallenging when you are checking back and not driven by your own emotional reactions.

I CAN ALWAYS CHECK IF I UNDERSTAND OTHER PEOPLE'S COMMUNICATIONS CLEARLY

The second kind of converting is done when you are converting information so you can understand a person's root communication but you do not need to check back or reply to them. Out of the millions of pieces of information you receive there are some that do not require responses and you need to use your judgement as to what the root communication was. Remember other people's communications are not always directed at you and may in some cases simply be an externalisation of their thought processes. There are some people you encounter in your life with whom you may not want or need to get involved.

The third kind of converting can take place when you extract information from incoming communications and it becomes apparent that those communications contain negative, destructive information. However, all communications contain information about other people and the world around you so you can learn something from everything, even if it is only to avoid certain circumstances. You can convert the communication you receive into useful information that can help you negotiate the world more easily.

The fourth kind of converting takes place as you learn to speak in other people's communication styles. This requires you to study the way other people communicate and demands you learn many different ways of communicating so you can confidently match other people's communication styles.

Modelling Excellence

There are three basic methods by which we learn. The first is constructing an action from external information such as learning to compose music from a book. The second is experiential learning when we are doing a task, getting feedback from our actions and then knowing how to do that task a second time. The third and quickest method is modelling, which is copying what someone else is doing.

Whenever you want to do something, find someone who already knows how to do that task well. It does not matter what the task is. It could be linguistics, photoreading (reading 25,000 word per minute) or relaxation, absolutely anything at all. Talk to the person who knows how to do the task, analyse them, ask them how they do that task, copy them, walk like them, talk like them, think like them and be them. This way you will be able to model the function they are performing...going on from there...when you have managed to replicate their behaviour, then change that behaviour so it produces the best results for you.

Cue Confidence

Confidence is about the way you walk, talk, sit, stand, breathe, eat, drink, think, act and feel about yourself and your adapted orientation to your own ever changing environment, or not as the case may be. There are a lot of things happening at the same time so there is a need to be able to instantly recall the good mechanisms and feelings you have learnt when you are confidently putting them into action all at the same time.

To gain instant access to this state of confidence you can use a cue that will suddenly give you all those abilities all at once. The cue can be a word, sound, image, feeling, smell, taste, posture, touching an area on your body or a combination of all of those things. You then use that cue whenever you need to be confident.

I remember the great English character actress Beryl Reid talking about how she built up her characters for her performances. She said each character started with a pair of shoes and as she got to know the shoes the different aspects of the character's personality got added on. When she was in a film or a play all she had to do was put on the shoes and she would automatically go into character.

After a while, as you practise, the cue begins to happen automatically out of your conscious awareness and you find that you are confident without consciously having to try. In reading this you can remember the four-stage process of competence that we talked about earlier, consisting of unconscious incompetence, conscious incompetence, conscious competence and unconscious competence.

Installing Confidence (Script)

Installing a confidence cue is an easy thing for me to do...being able to add to my communication abilities with myself...***WITH MY EYES CLOSED I CAN RELAX AND IMAGINE THE PROCESS IN TRANCE***...going to a place in time when I was really confident I can remember all the ways I was...in my mind I can replicate that experience to its strongest degree...***I ATTACH THE EXPERIENCE TO A CUE OF MY CHOOSING NOW!***...moving on to a time and place when I was at peace with myself I can experience those good sensations ...immersed in that wonderful experience I can intensify it to the maximum ...***I ATTACH THAT PEACE TO MY CONFIDENCE CUE NOW!***...moving on to a time and place of great happiness I can experience those good sensations ...fully experiencing those feelings and bodily experiences of good humour to the maximum...***I CAN ATTACH THAT HAPPINESS TO MY CONFIDENCE CUE NOW!***...these three important constituents of confidence can be inseparably linked together in my mind...whenever I access the confidence cue I will re-experience those compounded good states as confidence...***I CAN FIX THE GOOD STATE OF CONFIDENCE WITH THE CUE IN MY MIND NOW!***

Some people reach this good state of confidence in light trance in one session; however, the more you use it the stronger it becomes, compounding its effects and your ability to act and react in a confident way. In chapter eight I discussed a great deal about creating *foundation states* and how to use them. It will serve you well to install the peace state at the beginning and constantly into your confidence-creating actions that start with peace, and notice the huge increase in your calm, controlled level of confidence.

Collapsing in New Elements

If you want to fold in new experiences, then as you go through the installation processes in your mind, add extra elements like an internal cinema screen that is continuously showing how you act and feel confidently, leaving it running constantly, whether you are awake or asleep.

Add smells, tastes, sounds, music, peace, happiness and songs for confidence, internally in your mind and in your actions through post-hypnotic self-suggestion. Allow all those elements to compound together to form the new stronger state of confidence.

LIKE A GREAT AND BEAUTIFUL PIECE OF ART THE STATE OF MY CONFIDENCE CAN BE A LIVING WORK OF ART IN ITSELF

Throughout your life you can continually fold in new elements to your personality and experiences since you are flesh, blood, mind and spirit, with nothing set in stone. What you can also do is eradicate parts of the confidence cue that do not suit you anymore – repair, install new mechanisms, even folding in stronger intensities of experience. Change the colour, hue, strength, texture, contrast, loudness, softness and intensity of your internal experiences so they in turn reflect your new state of mind in your behaviour or the new behaviours you are installing.

I CAN REMEMBER IMAGINATION IS THE KEY WORKING FROM THE INSIDE OUTWARDS

Imagining Success

Some people say:

Well I don't know what it is like to feel successful.
I have never been successful.
I cannot imagine what it is like to be successful.
Would I be here if I knew what it was like to be successful?

My response is very simple to such statements and questions. If you can imagine and experience what it is like to be unconfident, then automatically you do know what your images of success are, because if you did not, you would not know *unsuccessful*. You must know both to be able to make a comparison.

I CAN REMEMBER MY IMAGINATION IS THE KEY

If you can imagine something you are halfway there to achieving it because you can study that imagined image. Break it down into smaller, replicable elements, modelling each of those parts, and then rebuild the parts back up into a whole behavioural routine.

Rehearsal

Many of the things you do in your life you have rehearsed a thousand times – walking, making tea, speaking, 10 times table, driving a car, and smiling at your granny. Rehearsal is practice that can take place both in the real world and in your mind, just like when you learnt a poem.

I CAN REGULARLY INSTALL A SENSE OF AND MECHANISM FOR CONFIDENCE IN MYSELF

If you do the rehearsals inside your head when you want to be confident, while you are in trance, then when you come to do the behaviour or task in reality it will seem automatic. This is what we call installation of automatic responses. Practice breeds familiarity.

Attitude

Remember, confidence is not arrogance so it must have a sense of peace at its core. Also, whatever you do well needs to be something you enjoy on some level, whether you are a heart surgeon, grave digger, police officer, window cleaner or defusing a nuclear bomb.

NUMBER ONE RULE OF LIFE – LET IT BE FUN!

Tape record and video yourself, carefully analysing the way you are performing confidence. Note what changes you can make and then devise the kind of positive affirmations and scripts you need to make to yourself during trance to get those changes to happen.

Focus and Concentration

When people say they cannot do something it is usually because they have not applied themselves to the task. When you apply yourself to the task you can be surprised at how competent you can be. We are all learning all the time throughout our lives about how to have confidence in different situations, and in order to pay attention to the process, we need to focus and concentrate.

I CAN CONFIDENTLY FOCUS AND CONCENTRATE ON CONFIDENCE AND THE TASK IN HAND

As I say many times in this work we are all much more capable than we give ourselves credit for at a conscious level. Again you can suggest to yourself that you concentrate on the communication in hand when you are in a communication with someone else.

Philosophical Basis to Life

Each of us travel our own journey through life and it would be arrogant of me to tell you which philosophy to travel with as I do not walk your walk or talk your talk. Whether you are a Christian, atheist, humanitarian, Muslim, Pagan or communist is your own decision that you can come to as you learn about life and study the way you believe life best works for you and those around you.

Confidence is best supported by a mind that has discovered philosophical guidelines to live by that do not prejudge the self or those around you for their beliefs or lack of them. It is so easy for us to become pious when we think we have the answers to life which is, after all, simply a matter of ever changing questions and answers.

ONE POWER OF MY CONFIDENCE CAN BE IN KINDNESS

You can do confidence with kindness and care for others, remembering that although you need to start with yourself the world is not only about you. Success and money can, in some ways, give you freedom to live life on your own terms but the success you need to find to live life happily is the accepting and excelling of your own personality and your place in the world.

I CAN LEAVE THE WORLD A BETTER PLACE THAN I FOUND IT ...RESPECTING NATURE

Remember the story of King Midas – everything he touched turned to gold and eventually he touched his beloved daughter who became gold and was his daughter no more.

The Good Morning Smile

Some years ago when I was in America I learnt how to smile when greeting people. The sales conference was run by a man who taught me the difference between smiling and smiling. Many people, when they greet someone, smile with the top half of their face frozen and this portrays an unconscious message to the other person that they do not really mean the greeting but are faking politeness. It shows the communicator is holding back and when the English do this it is referred to as the stiff upper lip.

I CAN GENUINELY THINK HOW I CAN ENRICH THE OTHER PERSON'S EXPERIENCE THROUGH MY CONFIDENT COMMUNICATION

A genuine greeting causes the top half the face to come alive as the nerves from the zygomatic area around the cheekbones send a message to the centre of the brain that produces happy hormones. Your eyes are also the window to your soul and the person opposite you can tell, at an unconscious level, whether you are getting the happiness feeling when you are communicating with them. When you greet someone, let your whole face light up and be genuine in your communication with them and they will respond positively if you have learnt the skills of communication well.

Confidently Learning and Reflecting Confidence (Script)

The work I put in on learning how to be a confident person can pay off a thousand fold...it is a truth that I am what I make myself to be...***LIKE A GREAT AND BEAUTIFUL PIECE OF ART THE STATE OF MY CONFIDENCE IS A LIVING WORK IN ITSELF***...becoming what I need...want or desire to be...working out the strategies to make that happen...***I CAN REMEMBER MY IMAGINATION IS THE KEY***...since the brain is a living organism it will constantly need feeding...what it needs feeding is a process of ongoing research into myself...***I CAN REGULARLY INSTALL A SENSE OF AND MECHANISMS FOR CONFIDENCE IN MYSELF***...including joy into the process of learning about...installing...and doing confidence...there will always be the choice to take a path of suffering...***NUMBER ONE RULE OF LIFE – LET IT BE FUN***...focusing on my ability to recreate myself every day...taking each step at a time...***I CAN CONFIDENTLY FOCUS AND CONCENTRATE ON CONFIDENCE AND THE TASK IN HAND***...some people do not know of positive construction...they have a distance to travel on their own journey...***ONE POWER OF CONFIDENCE CAN BE IN KINDNESS***...the Native Americans believe they are the caretakers of the land and not the owners...philosophically my confidence can arise from my respect for myself ...other beings and the world around me...***I CAN LEAVE THE WORLD A BETTER PLACE THAN I FOUND IT***...***RESPECTING NATURE***...the responsibility for my communications lies solely with me...the building and rebuilding of my confidence is mine...***I CAN GENUINELY THINK HOW I CAN ENRICH THROUGH MY CONFIDENT COMMUNICATIONS***...it is OK to be an individual...basing my actions on careful aforethought and consideration for myself and others...***I WILL BE MORE CONFIDENT AS MY THOUGHTS AND ACTIONS ARE BALANCED***...communication...kindness...and consideration are as much part of my skills as reading other people's communications ...making my own communications clear and succinct...***I AM CONFIDENT AND WILL REFLECT THAT TO OTHERS WHO FEEL GOOD ABOUT MY CONFIDENCE***.

Summary

■ Acquiring confidence ability skills through learning about the way communications work with your body language and voice.

■ Installing a cue for confidence, learning to read other people's communications and make sure yours are succinct.

■ Consider how self-image is formed and able to be changed by using screening, filtering, analysing and converting.

■ Organising your time management so that you can apply yourself exclusively to a task and allow that task to have your full attention.

■ Operate the formula:

$$EFFORT\ (E) + TIME\ (T) + TECHNIQUE\ (TE) = RESULTS + SELF\ TRADEMARK®$$

■ Seek out those who do a task you wish to do well and model them, fine-tuning the end result to your own needs.

■ Imagine success, whatever that means to you, rehearse it in your own head in trance using focus and concentration.

■ Greet the world with your good morning smile and the likelihood is that the majority of the world will want to do the same to you.

■ Do the exercises on p161 and p175.

Frequently Asked Questions

Q. My boss at work has always frightened the life out of me with her four degrees, high powered decision-making style, and living in the very best part of town. What trance can I do to give me more confidence with her?

A. Don't assume that all is as you have seen it. You may only be seeing part of her life and you may be projecting your fears of failure onto her success which will make the gap seem wider. Learn a great deal more about how to communicate with her. Remember, confidence is about the chatter that is going on in your own mind and not in other people's. Accept constructive criticism, address it by devising a trance to change things. But most of all use your body and your mind together in co-ordination to present the ideal image of yourself you create...FROM THE INSIDE OUTWARDS.

Q. You talk about screening, filtering, analysing, and converting incoming communications but doesn't that take a lot of time and make the spontaneity go out of a communication?

A. As you install those mechanisms in trance to become automatic you can change your sense of time in your head so that your mind time is longer than real time. Slow the time down inside your head so you have all the time you need but your responses seem spontaneous. Of course you can set the speed of your own communications to suit yourself. Take your time to listen, watch, think and expound communications to positively construct something that is generally a pleasurable and enriching experience for all. Investigate the ideas of empathy and reciprocity.

Q. Sometimes I have all the confidence in my mind but when I open my mouth I babble. What can I do?

A. Slow everything down so you gain control and see the words as they come out of your mouth, giving them shape and colour in your mind to reflect their meaning. Practise singing the things you want to say in the privacy of your own home – this really helps people who come to me with a stutter.

Q. If I do hypnosis and communication skills every day, how long will it take before I will be totally confident?

A. Very quickly as you are being POSITIVE ACTIVE and taking control of your life. However, remember that confidence is like a dance – it is progressive and very different every time. I am one of the most confident people I know because I am always installing new programmes in myself and most of all I have a belief that I love spending time with people of all kinds.

Q. If there is a time when I suffer a crisis of confidence and suddenly panic and go back into old patterns of being nervous, what can I do?
*A. Take a moment and sit to one side, going into a trance and calming yourself down. Look at the internal picture that you have running which depicts how you are when you are confident and check out the elements that are making you confident in that internal representation of yourself. Then copy externally exactly what the confident internal representation is doing. Access your cues for confidence and...**BE AN ACTOR**.*

Further Reading

BERNE, ERIC, MD, **WHAT DO YOU SAY AFTER YOU SAY HELLO?** CORGI BOOKS, CA, USA, 1974.

BOLTON, ROBERT, PhD, **PEOPLE SKILLS**, TOUCHSTONE, SIMON & SCHUSTER, NEW YORK, 1986.

BOURNE, EDMUND J, **THE ANXIETY AND PHOBIA WORKBOOK**, NEW HARBINGER PUBLICATIONS, CA, USA, 1995.

CARNEGIE, DALE, **HOW TO WIN FRIENDS AND INFLUENCE PEOPLE**, VERMILLION, LONDON, 1998.

COLEMAN, VERNON, **PEOPLE WATCHING**, BLUE BOOKS, DEVON, UK, 1995.

GILBERT, PAUL, **OVERCOMING DEPRESSION**, ROBINSON PUBLISHING, LONDON, 1997.

KNIGHT, SUE, **NLP SOLUTIONS: HOW TO MODEL WHAT WORKS IN BUSINESS TO MAKE IT WORK FOR YOU**, NICHOLAS BREALEY PUBLISHING, LONDON, 1999.

LABORDE, GENIE Z, **INFLUENCING WITH INTEGRITY: MANAGEMENT SKILLS FOR COMMUNICATION & NEGOTIATION**, ANGLO AMERICAN BOOK CO, CA, USA, 1987.

MCKAY, MATTHEW, **SELF-ESTEEM**, NEW HARBINGER PUBLICATIONS, CA, USA, 1992.

MALTZ, MAXWELL & SOMMER, BOBBE, **PSYCHO-CYBERNETICS 2000**, PRENTICE HALL, NEW JERSEY, USA, 1993.

O'CONNOR, JOSEPH & SEYMOUR, JOHN, **INTRODUCING NLP: NEURO-LINGUISTIC PROGRAMMING**, THE AQUARIAN PRESS, CA, USA, 1990.

PEASE, ALLAN, **BODY LANGUAGE: HOW TO READ OTHERS' THOUGHTS BY THEIR GESTURES**, SHELDON PRESS, LINCOLN, UK, 1981.

ROBBINS, ANTHONY, **UNLIMITED POWER**, SIMON & SCHUSTER, LONDON, 1988.

SALTER, BRIAN & LANGFORD-WOOD, NAOMI, **SUCCESSFULLY DEALING WITH DIFFICULT PEOPLE IN A WEEK**, HODDER & STOUGHTON, LONDON, 1998.

THOMSON, KEVIN, **PASSION AT WORK: SIX SECRETS FOR PERSONAL SUCCESS**, CAPSTONE PUBLISHING, OXFORD, UK, 1998.

WHITESIDE, ROBERT L, **FACE LANGUAGE: A GUIDE TO MEETING THE RIGHT PERSON**, LIFETIME BOOKS, FLORIDA, USA, 1992.

Chapter Ten

Self-Hypnosis for Life

Having a skill or ability and knowing how to apply it are two different matters. As you go on to learn more about self-hypnosis and how it can be of use in your life you will become more empowered as a human being. Certain things are sure as we move into the third millennium, which will shape many of our lives. More than two thirds of the world's population are now living in cities where the quality of their life is often of a low standard. People can suffer separation from close relatives and friends, poverty, intense loneliness and depression.

The illnesses and diseases of developed, industrialised or post-industrial/technological societies are very different from undeveloped pre-industrial cultures. Mental illness, depression and feelings of being out of control of your life will be among the greatest distresses of the 21st century. Not only has big brother arrived in the form of the police state but so has the corporate culture, with some multi-national firms having a larger annual income than some countries as they dominate our lives.

In order to feel good about yourself in the future it will be necessary to gain, retain, and regain a deep sense of being in control of your own life, body, state of mind and spiritual development, whatever that means to you. Those who cannot do that will be sucked into the mire of automatons who will eat, sleep and work repetitively without ever questioning the quality of their lives.

As the technological revolution arrived it gave access to knowledge throughout the world to a class of people who previously had not had a chance of an extensive education or personal development. It is now possible to seek out learning for a small amount of money anywhere in the developed world to become whatever you want to be. For the undeveloped world it will still be a struggle to survive against the elements, hunger, disease and particularly western world domination.

In a world like I have described it is increasingly important to have a discipline of mind to help you live peacefully, adventurously, adaptively and charitably. Many of the techniques in this book will help you do those things very successfully; however, remember above all else, it is not what I can do for you, but what you are willing to do for yourself.

Let this work be merely a stepping stone for you across the stream of life that leads you to further investigations as you seek out more books about self-hypnosis and personal development. It is your brain...***USE IT***...***AGAIN***...***AND AGAIN***...***AND AGAIN***...***OR LOSE IT***.

Apart from what you have learnt so far, hypnosis can also be used for pain control, anaesthesia, advanced learning techniques, getting rid of phobias, sexual enhancement, family therapy and many other applications, all of which, due to space, I was unable to cover in this book. Each can be taught to a person so they can induce those phenomena through self-hypnosis.

Today as I was writing this chapter I got a telephone call from a woman who was 5ft 4 inches tall and 14 stone in weight. These proportions are medically dangerous because she was undoubtedly obese and causing damage to her heart and other organ functions, which will probably mean early death and possibly psychological problems in her life.

The first thing she asked me was how much it would cost to come and see me. I immediately knew I would not take her as a client because she had failed to ask me if I could help her or indicated to me that she wanted help to become a healthy weight. It was obvious that she was not happy at the present weight otherwise she would not have telephoned me. The intonation I caught in her voice told me that she believed I should do all the work for her to lose the weight and she would not continue in treatment if she consciously did not like what was happening.

The truth is this woman was not ready to lose weight and no therapist or doctor in the world would have been able to help her until she decided that she wanted help. There is little point dragging a thirsty camel to the sea if it only drinks fresh water.

I believe that your abilities are far more than you are presently consciously aware of, but at the end of the day it does not matter a fig what I think: if you do not do the work with yourself to change your mind, body, life and future, nothing will happen.

Pills are rarely the answer to depression or insomnia but many medical practitioners will give them to you recklessly just to get rid of you because they have a waiting room full of patients. Many of the people who are in hospital beds are there because of the side effects of their prescribed medication. Electric shock treatment does not solve the problems of the extremely depressed patient, but psychiatrists are still administering this barbaric procedure; in fact it often devastates the lives of so many victims who have ended up with little memories of their previous life.

When depression and insomnia arrive it is generally because your unconscious has a message for you and it is trying to get you to pay attention to what it is saying. Something is wrong in your life or you should be doing something specific that you are not, so your unconscious is trying to get you to consciously realise what that is and do something about it. Go into a trance and ask your unconscious to let you know what is wrong and what you can constructively do to go forward in a **POSITIVE ACTIVE** manner so that your circumstances will change and improve.

Having gone through that process and worked out consciously what you need to do, devise a trance script to suggest to yourself what you can do to help you go forward. Learn the script, turning parts of it into a mantra and use it in trance at least once a day. If your circumstances are very difficult or if you want immediate change, use the trance three or several times a day to accelerate the change in your psyche and consequently your life.

REMEMBER...I CAN BE MY OWN HERO OR HEROINE

Some years ago a friend of mine who is a psychiatrist in Derby telephoned me to ask if I would see a 68-year-old man called Ben who was extremely depressed. The psychiatrist did not know what to do with Ben as he had offered him antidepressants for a year but Ben had refused them.

Ben told me how he had worked for 55 years in the same mill, even during the war when he had helped keep the mill running, turning out khaki for the soldiers' uniforms. His wife had died and eventually the mill gave him a gold watch on his 65th birthday, retired him, and thanked him for his service.

His mates had offered to take him to the pub with them and play darts but he hated smoky pubs. The women from the mill had offered to take him to Bingo with them, but he did not fancy that either. When his daughter suggested he lived with them by the sea, where they had a nice view for him to look at, he told them he was retired, not dead.

When I taught him self-hypnotic dreaming some weeks later he decided to enrol at the local technical college for engineering to keep an eye on his wayward grandson. He also used self-hypnosis during his studies to give him the confidence to outperform people 50 years younger than himself. Eventually he got a PhD and was employed as a consultant to the many mills in the north of England where he had known the owners' fathers, grandfathers, and great grandfathers.

Taking control of your life and determining your own future is something most people have been taught not to do since their very early childhood by schools, governments, employers and most of all advertisers. Go inside into a trance and ask your unconscious to let you know what you really want from life because it is often something other than you are currently settling for.

If you want to be another Leonardo Da Vinci, go inside and work out how to do that. If your dream is to give up all your material comforts and become an eco warrior, find a strategy that can help you do that and still be safe in your dotage. Never ask if I can do this but:

HOW CAN I DO WHATEVER I NEED...WANT...OR DESIRE

When you are aware of a nagging, doubting voice inside your head that is warning you not to do what you are proposing, go into a trance and talk to that voice. It will be part of you that has something really important to say, so listen to it and consider how you can satisfy its needs as well. The part of you that errs on the side of caution is, after all, only doing its job to protect you, but do not let it become overbearing and stand in your way, nor ignore it because it has a right to take part in the whole process of living. Work with it, talk to it and negotiate to satisfy its needs.

Stuart came to me suffering from prescription drug addiction. When he was 16 his parents argued and made so much noise that he could never get any sleep. His doctor prescribed sleeping pills and kept prescribing them so that by the time Stuart was 23 he was addicted to them. This was further complicated by the fact that he had started to take cocaine, go out to raves and take Ecstasy at the weekends.

While many people experiment with recreational drugs in their youth, by far the majority of them do not get hooked. Because Stuart was already an addict when he started to play with recreational drugs, he was unable to handle the highs and lows, ending up in a psychotic state of mind with high anxiety and insomnia. The sad thing is that the psychiatrist who treated him never tested him for drugs but simply prescribed more drugs to try to help him sleep. By the time he came to me, he rattled with the amount of medication that he was taking.

With self-hypnosis he was able to learn to control his behaviour, moods, diet, take physical exercise and learn to induce calm states and reduce his medication dramatically.

Some people can spend years becoming highly educated achievers in their own particular fields and never feel confident about what they do, even though it appears to everyone that they are in complete control. They have managed to fake their public image on the outside and are in constant fear of being found out for being a fraud. The thing is they really have no need to be afraid about their talents because they are often very good at what they do. Although many times other people have praised them, they never seem to quite believe those opinions.

Anton at 35 had an MD and was an assistant professor of medicine, whose work earned him tremendous respect. For a boy that came from the slums of a third world country who arrived in England with absolutely nothing but the clothes he stood up in, he had done tremendously well. Everyone thought what a nice chap he was and how his kindness helped a lot of his medical students beyond the call of his job.

In his country of origin, things had been very difficult for him as a child because his father had been a well-known right-wing extremist responsible for many of the deaths of people in his home town. After his father died, the family had lived in absolute poverty and terror, being shunned and stoned by the locals, even having had their house burnt down. England had not only been a chance for a better life but somewhere where no one had known anything about his family history. All his life there had been a voice in his head that had called him the dirty son of a murdering fascist.

Only when he learnt about the safe space imagery did he feel sufficiently confident to face his own inner feelings about himself. It was a surprise to him that his own internal image of himself was so bad that he believed he did not deserve his success.

Only after constantly installing new beliefs about himself in trance, facing the internalised voices that denigrated him, and installing new internal tapes and inner mind pictures, did he begin for the first time in his life to like the person he had become. It was even more shocking to him that he found after a few months that he even liked the person he had always been, even though he had been punishing himself for his father's actions.

We spend so much time in our lives trying to make sense of the outside world in which we live that we forget that our inside world is just as big and resourceful. There are times when we find ourselves completely alone facing deep tragedies that we may feel have been foisted on us. We are stripped of the paraphenalia of modern social living, consumerism and peer approval or disapproval and have to rely on what we have become, learnt about ourselves and use our self-management skills to get from one day to the next.

Fiona had been raised in an extremely wealthy family, had all the privileges of wealth, education and position. She was the only child of one of Europe's wealthiest aristocrats and had never worked; instead she flitted around the globe, yearly passing through Monte Carlo, New York, Paris, London, and Jamaica.

She was jet set, with cocaine, Gucci luggage, private limousines and yachts. At 27 a diagnosis of HIV positive led her to rethink her life and how she could get to 30, never mind any further. Her main problem was that in order to change her life she had to abandon a lot of her previous friends because nearly everyone she had been mixing with was also using cocaine, constantly travelling and sleeping around.

Each day in self-hypnosis she spent time with a duplicated self so that she would always have someone to be her friend and watch over her. Her second self was her constant companion, giving her lots of hugs and loving, which was something she had never really experienced from anyone. Several times a day for the first three months she went into a trance and worked on her immune system by visualising the white blood cells and getting them to attack the HIV

137

virus. Another visualisation she used was to strengthen her T-cell count which is the part of the blood system that is knocked out by the virus.

She began to work as a fundraiser for a charity that ships medical supplies out to Africa to fight the HIV epidemic. She also visited Africa to work as a volunteer at the grassroots level in slums and shanty towns, trying as much as she could to share her life with others who were also HIV positive or who had developed AIDS. The last time I heard from her she told me that she was happier and more fulfilled than she had ever been in her life.

Decision Making

Throughout our lives we are faced daily with decisions about major and minor issues that shape our present and future. Sometimes we can be unsure about which is the right decision to make in order to get the best outcome from our present situation or how to choose from several options that may face us as we go forward.

The wrong decision or indecision can have effects that range from inconvenient to disastrous. However, we are only human and that means we can simply do the best with what we have and know at any particular point in time. In retrospect it is easy for anyone to think perhaps if I had done it differently I might have got a better result, but since we made that decision, it is necessary for us to know that we did the very best we could with the information we had.

The Decision-Making Tree (Script)

As I rest in trance I can find myself at the roots of a problem which is concerned with making a decision...there are choices to be made and options to be considered...***I AM CAPABLE OF MAKING WELL THOUGHT OUT GOOD DECISIONS***...sitting on the trunk of the decision-making tree I can see the options before me as many different branches...some may be mundane choices and others can be outrageous whilst there may be middle ways as well...***I CAN SEE ALL THE DIFFERENT OPTIONS BRANCHING OUT BEFORE ME***...at the end of each branch can be the goal I seek to attain...as I travel along the first branch I can work out the acceptable principles by which I may operate to reach my goal...***I CAN CONSIDER MY VALUES...BELIEFS...AND ATTITUDES AS THEY REFLECT THE ACCEPTABILITY OF THIS BRANCH OF ACHIEVING MY GOAL***...what are the strategies and actions I must undertake to make that goal happen...do those strategies and actions co-ordinate with my values...attitudes and beliefs...***IT IS A GOOD FEELING TO CONSIDER WHETHER MY INTEGRITY WILL STAY IN TACT***...having reached my goal is the place as good as I thought it would be...travelling beyond the goal and looking backwards at what happened due to that goal being achieved...***I CAN CONSIDER THE EFFECTS***

THAT THE ACHIEVED GOAL HAD ON MY LIFE AND OTHERS...am I comfortable with the place I am at and feelings I am having...returning back to the root of the problems it is possible to see that other branches offer different directions to reaching my goal or even different goals if I desire ...*TAKING THE NEXT BRANCH I CAN AGAIN CONSIDER THE GOAL... VALUES...BELIEFS...ATTITUDES...ACTIONS...STRATEGIES AND RESULTS* ...my unconscious with its vast resources will help guide me in my exploration of the options...the time inside my head is far greater than real time and allows me to have the luxury of slowing the whole process down...*I CAN COMPARE THE TWO OPTIONS IN MY MIND FROM THE PLACE THAT IS BEYOND REACHING THE GOAL AS I LOOK BACKWARDS AT THEIR EFFECTS*...as I return to the root of the problem I can rest and ponder whether I wish to explore other branches or other options...*RESTING COM-FORTABLY IN TRANCE I CAN CONSIDER ALL THE OPTIONS I NEED*...my unconscious can choose the best way for me to go forward that is the most empathic to my life course...if I need to my unconscious can create new branches to satisfy that need...*I WILL BECOME AWARE OF THE BEST WAY FORWARD FOR ME BOTH IN THE SHORT AND LONG TERM*...(Allow 10 minutes if you are recording a tape for the process to take place)...as I am aware of the decision that I have made it can feel good...knowing that it is the best decision I could have made...*I WILL COMFORTABLY TAKE MEA-SURES TO IMPLEMENT THAT DECISION FROM NOW!*

Having found the decision that is right for you, sometimes it is a good thing to look at that decision consciously by drawing the structure of the decision on a large piece of paper in coloured pens like a piece of art. Then go back to looking at self-affirmations and design your own script for installing whatever new attitudes and strategies you need to follow that decision through.

Resources from the Future

Many philosophers and psychologists often talk about the different stages of life and how we develop our own particular human experiences along similar courses. Firstly the growing child is motivated to go out into the world, learning, expanding their territory and eventually reproducing in adulthood. The motivation that drives us forward compels us to seek out people who are similar to ourselves to commune with, share experience, and compare ourselves against.

Around 40 plus onwards most people find that they have to reassess their lives as they come to the end of the average breeding cycle and enter into middle age. Children grow up and people are left to face what they are going to do with the rest of their lives. What may have been satisfactory as they were raising families often no longer seems enough to satisfy the mature mind. In old age people frequently begin to die around you and you are faced with having to deal with who and what you have been, are now, and will be as you realise that life will not go on forever.

If when you get to old age you find you have led a wonderful, satisfying, rewarding and contributing life then everything is just fine. However, many people wake up one day at 70 and are horrified at the life they have led, people they have been, and opportunities they have missed.

Resources from the Future (Script)

As I rest inside I can leave my body in a safe place…with my eyes closed I can enjoy going deeper into a wonderful trance…***BEING AWARE MY MIND AND BODY CAN OPERATE INDEPENDENTLY***…leaving my body behind I can travel forward into my future…sitting upon the large throne of success that marks the end of my life…***I GREET RESPECTFULLY THE WISER OLD PERSON I HAVE BECOME***…knowing that knowledge…wisdom…hindsight and clarity emerge from experience…sharing the throne with the person I have become and who has the knowledge of having lived my life…***I CAN ASK FOR THE RESOURCES I NEED TO TAKE BACK TO MY LIFE***… including love…knowledge…wisdom…kindness…patience…bravery and a spirit of adventure…each time I take a resource it magically duplicates so all the original resources remain in place in the future…***I CAN FILL A HUGE CONTAINER WITH ALL THE RESOURCES I WILL NEED TO LIVE MY LIFE***…those resources can have sound…colour…shape…texture…weight …feeling…smell…taste…they will carry every dimension and content that I need to live my life well…***I CAN USE ALL THOSE RESOURCES TO FILL MY LIFE WITH THE MANY SKILLS I NEED…AND TO BE MYSELF WELL***…as I sit with my wise old self for a while hugging them…thank you is my parting greeting…for each version of myself I meet in every timeframe of my existence on the way back I will give them resources…***EACH AND EVERY PART OF ME IN EVERY TIMEFRAME WILL BE MORE ENRICHED AND RESOURCEFUL***…yet again every time I use a resource it magically replicates so I will never run out of all the resources I need…and as I settle back down into my body peace surrounds me…***I ACCEPT THAT I AM THE MAGICIAN WITHIN FOREVER…AND EVER.***

The world is a wonderful place filled with so many fantastic things to see and splendid people to meet. Let life fill you with joy and sunshine. Be not afraid that you will fail at the things you attempt; take life by the handlebars and ride until you reach your destination, whatever that may be.

Take each day at a time and plan meticulously your strategy for a better life, world and future, using your self-hypnosis time to help you do that calmly and efficiently. Remember that there are things that are beyond your control and being adaptable and flexible are the essential qualities that enable you to change your life, the world, and avoid the pitfalls so you can make it to the end of your physical life.

Take the techniques and messages within this work and build them into your life, going from success to success. Never forget, however, that there are those who are much less fortunate than you who do not have the abilities that are needed to pursue excellence at this moment in time. They have a journey to travel and we should not judge them for their inability but praise them for their abilities, encouraging them to aspire to be their very best...let kindness be your byword (see the exercises on p163 and p174).

Desire...aspire and conspire for your own sense of excellence...you are all and more than you ever dreamed you could be, using what you know...

...SELF-HYPNOSIS FOR LIFE...

Further Reading

BOYERS, ROBERT, **LAING AND ANTI-PSYCHIATRY**, PENGUIN BOOKS, UK, 1971.

BREGGIN, PETER R, MD, **TALKING BACK TO PROZAC: WHAT DOCTORS AREN'T TELLING YOU ABOUT TODAY'S MOST CONTROVERSIAL DRUG**, ST MARTIN'S PRESS, NEW YORK, 1994.

BREGGIN, PETER R, MD, **TOXIC PSYCHIATRY, DRUGS & ELECTRO-CONVULSIVE THERAPY: THE TRUTH & THE BETTER ALTERNATIVES**, HARPER COLLINS, LONDON, 1993.

DEARLOVE, DES, **BUSINESS THE RICHARD BRANSON WAY: 10 SECRETS OF THE WORLD'S GREATEST BRAND-BUILDER**, CAPSTONE PUBLISHING, OXFORD, UK, 1998.

HARRIS, AMY & HARRIS, THOMAS, **STAYING OK**, ARROW BOOKS, LONDON, 1985.

MOORE, THOMAS J, **PRESCRIPTION FOR DISASTER: THE HIDDEN DANGERS IN YOUR MEDICINE CABINET**, SIMON & SCHUSTER, NEW YORK, 1998.

WYBURD, GILES, **COMPETITIVE & ETHICAL? HOW BUSINESS CAN STRIKE A BALANCE**, KOGAN PAGE, LONDON, 1998.

YAPKO, MICHAEL D, PhD, **HAND ME DOWN BLUES: HOW TO STOP DEPRESSION FROM SPREADING IN FAMILIES**, GOLDEN BOOKS, NEW YORK, 1999.

Useful Organisations for Practitioners of Ethical Research in Medicine
Doctors and Lawyers for Responsible Medicine, 104B Weston Park, London N8 9PP.

Dr Hadwen Trust for Humane Research, 84A Tilehouse Street, Hitchin, Herts SG5 2DY. Website http://www.drhadwentrust.org.uk

Physician's Committee for Responsible Medicine, 5100 Wisconsin Avenue, NW, Suite 404, Washington DC 20016, USA. Website http://www.pcrm.org

Afterword

As you get to the end of this book on self-hypnosis I hope it is only the beginning for you and that you will use trance states each day, enjoying deep rest and contemplation, which adds considerably to the living experience. Whenever you need to you can take this book back off the shelf to consult it on ways to change or explore your psyche. Make up scripts and use your experiences of dealing with life on your own terms, feeling you have control, and are not afraid of losing control when the time is right. Go out and buy other books on self-hypnosis and add their knowledge to your collection.

Most of all, be not afraid to be adventurous in your own mind, exploring, developing and changing the contents of your unconscious so that you can get anything you need, want or desire. Your mind, body, emotional and spiritual experiences are your own to do with what you wish and let no one tell you otherwise. Finally, from the bottom of my heart I wish you to...*REMEMBER...THE NUMBER ONE RULE OF LIFE*...in everything you do...*LET IT BE FUN!*

BEHOLD THE HYPNOTIST WITHIN...

Glossary

Active: Taking control of your mind, body, emotions and life to determine what you will experience.

Abreaction: An uncomfortable and disturbing reaction that occurs when a person is in trance and is faced with an unpleasant experience. If this experience is very disturbing, a person should seek the help of a qualified hypnotherapist.

Active Stages: These are times when a person is acting out into the world.

Altered State: State of awareness that is other than consciousness but not sleep.

Attitudes: Behaviour that is guided by sets of values and beliefs.

Beliefs: A series of thought patterns that are regulators of behaviour based on values.

Brainwave Activity: The number of cycles per second at which the brain is oscillating. This includes different levels of High Beta, Beta, Alpha, Theta and Delta.

Catalepsy: When parts or the whole of the body is still and motionless as if frozen.

Centring: Bringing the awareness back into the present, paying immediate attention to your own needs and stabilising the personality.

Colour Tunnel Induction: An induction using a psycho-imaginary progressive colour changing scenario of travelling into a tunnel and progressively going deeper into trance.

Consciousness: Immediate awareness through all of the senses – visual, auditory, physical, feelings, smell, taste, emotional awareness and psychological thought processes.

Direct Imagery: Imagining a goal and being motivated to move directly towards that goal, trusting the unconscious to work out the details of the journey.

Disassociation: The perception of oneself as apart from the central personality, including the ability to look at oneself from a distance or to be consciously other than oneself.

Dissociative Window: A psycho-imaginary distancing from the individual during trance that allows them to see themselves analytically from a distance.

Emotions:
Positive Emotions: A sense of being psychologically, emotionally and physically comfortable with one's own sense of awareness.
Negative Emotions: A sense of being psychologically, emotionally and physically uncomfortable with one's own sense of awareness.
Neutral Emotions: Remaining directly unaffected by one's own present emotional state.
Overwhelming Emotions: Those emotions that are deemed inapplicable for the present level of experience.

Escalator Deepener: Psycho-imaginary technique using an escalator for taking oneself down into and up out of deep levels of trance.

External Respiration: Respiration through the lungs, exchanging carbon dioxide for oxygen.

False Memory Syndrome: The implementation of memories into the mind of a person that do not represent true events. These are imagined happenings.

Goal: A targeted achievement to work towards.

Habit Breaking: The cessation of unwanted behaviour and installation of wanted behaviour.

Helplessness: A giving up or inability to initiate one's own actions.

Hypnosis: The process by which an individual becomes self-absorbed and enters a trance-like altered state of awareness.

Hypnotherapy: The use of hypnosis alongside psychological disciplines to change thoughts, behaviours, emotions and experiences in co-ordination with a trained professional.

Hypnotic Re-Education: The implementation of new thoughts, mindsets, physical reactions and behaviours that are initiated within the trance experience. This can be carried out in light, mid or deep levels of trance. This can also be done in somnambulistic trance where the person appears not to be in trance experience but in fact is.

Hypnotic Governor: A series of suggestions that cause behaviour within certain margins.

Hypnotic Script: A written series of truth statements and suggestions which can be used to initiate thoughts, that can take a person into a trance, bring them back out of trance and initiate a change of psychology, physiology and behaviour.

Induction: The process by which a person is taken into a trance or takes themselves into trance. An induction can be achieved either through a person's own psychological thought processes or as a result of a hypnotist taking them into a trance-like state. Seeing a virtual reality in your own mind by creating images in the imagination.

Imagery: The internal representation of experiencing the five senses of sight, sound, feeling, smell and taste.

Imagination: The use of one's own psychological processes to create internal and alternative realities.

Internal Respiration: Oxygen going into the cells and waste products being taken away.

Interrupting Cues: A stimulus that occurs, indicating an unwanted behaviour.

Intra-Hypnotic Suggestion: A suggestion given during the trance experience to cause an action to happen within that trance.

Law of Delayed Effect: A suggestion given in trance causing an action to happen at a later time.

Meditation: A discipline of the mind from the East that requires concentration, an altered state of awareness and focusing within.

Metabolic Auto-Regulation: The ability of each organ to regulate its amount of oxygen and nutrition.

Mantra: A repetitive phrase constructed to form thought patterns and behaviour. The phrase may be chanted out loud, sub vocally or be a series of thoughts.

Mindsets: The structure and networks of thoughts that make up parts and structured ideas in the psyche both consciously and unconsciously.

Music Induction: The use of either real or imaginary music to take someone into a trance.

Natural Potential: One's innate or learned potential that may or may not be available to conscious awareness of one's life experiences and behaviours.

Negative Placebo Effect: An experience that is prevented from happening by belief and suggestion.

Negative Programming: The installation of thought structures in the psyche that cause certain behaviours, actions, reactions and emotions but which are psychologically detrimental to the individual.

Negative/Reactive: To react to a stimulus in a negative way.

Negative Reprogramming: The replacement or addition of new programmes to create psychological structures that cause certain behaviours, actions, reactions and emotions that are psychologically detrimental to the individual.

New Behaviour Installation: The installation of new behaviours in trance, not only to replace old ones, but also to initiate new thoughts or actions.

Now Exercise: Existential exercise that specifically draws a person's attention into the here and now to be aware of the constituents of existence.

Placebo Effect: An experience of something happening through belief and suggestion.

Personal Integrity: The cohesion of the personality, values, belief systems and attitudes that allows the individual to remain a whole personality with a positive view of themselves and the world.

Positive/Active: The outgoing motion responsible for initiating behaviour in a positive and constructive way.

Positive Affirmations: Thoughts, phrases, statements or actions that affirm or reaffirm a person's ability to act in a positive and competent way.

Post-Hypnotic Suggestion: A suggestion given during the trance experience that causes an action to happen after the trance experience.

Process Imagery: Progressive imaginings structured to take an individual towards a goal by sequential images, like going through a film, frame by frame.

Programming: The installation of psychological structures through suggestion that cause certain behaviours, actions, reactions and emotions.

Progressive Relaxation: The gradual relaxation of the body through the use of imaginative psychological techniques to see, hear and feel the body relaxing in stages.

Psyche: The whole experience of psychological and spiritual make-up.

Psychiatry: The medical branch of treating abnormal psychological behaviour.

Psycho-imaginary: Active imaginary techniques initiated by the individual themselves or by suggestion from a trained hypnotist or therapist.

Psychology: Discipline of examining thoughts, behaviours and emotional experience.

Raw Food Veganism: The branch of veganism where people eat only uncooked and unprocessed vegetables, legumes, fruit, nuts, and seeds.

Reactive: A physical, psychological or emotional behaviour that is initiated by a stimulus that is external or internal.

Regression: The process of unconsciously returning to your own past experiences while under hypnosis.

Repetition: Repeated implementation of thoughts, actions and psychological mechanisms to imprint or re-imprint behaviour and thought patterns.

Reprogramming: The replacement or addition of new programmes to create psychological structures that cause certain behaviours, actions, reactions and emotions.

Resting Stages: A time of contemplation and physical rest.

Safe Place Imagery: Being in a place in the mind where the individual feels protected from any threats, is safe, comfortable and at home within themselves.

Self-Empowerment: The psychological implementation of a good sense of one's own abilities. This can be a progressive, positive, constructive action, giving the person a high level of self-development.

Self-Hypnosis: The process by which a person takes themselves into a trance. Also known as auto-hypnosis.

Self-Suggestion: Suggestion used by a person both in and out of the trance-like state to cause an action to happen in the present or future.

Somnambulism: A waking sleep when a person seem to be conscious but is not fully aware of their surroundings. When this occurs during hypnosis it is referred to as artificial somnambulism.

Sound and Light Machine: Electrical device using binaural beats, listened to through headphones, and containing flashing lights in goggles that takes a person into altered states of awareness.

Stage Hypnotists: Entertainers who use hypnosis in order to amuse the public. This can be an extremely dangerous practice.

Stairs Deepener: Psycho-imaginary technique for deepening the trance experience using the image of stairs. The individual imagines that they are walking down or up the staircase.

Stressed: A person's sense of being in the flight or fight response when they are experiencing unnecessary stress that rightly belongs to another context.

Surfacing Memories: Those memories that have remained buried in the unconscious, which can surface at any time in a person's life and which can sometimes surface as a result of hypnosis.

Thought Stopping: The process by which one uses the concept of stopping to cease old thoughts and behaviours by positively using thoughts, words and actions that represent the concept of stop.

Trance: An altered state of awareness that is induced by hypnosis but can occur naturally, which is not sleep.

Trance Deepening: The process of going into a less conscious level of awareness during the trance experience.

Trance Dreaming: The ability of the mind to enter a dream-like state during hypnosis. This can be active (initiated by the individual's conscious or semi conscious) or passive dreaming, allowing the unconscious mind to determine the content of the dream.

Tumbling Trance: An induction into the trance-like state by rolling one's eyes backwards during a psycho-imaginary scenario of falling into a trance backwards.

Unconscious: Psychological and physiological processes that are activating outside of conscious awareness and not available to immediate awareness.

Unconscious Resources: The vast reservoir of abilities that one has accumulated during the course of a lifetime that are not constantly in conscious awareness but can be tapped into by allowing the unconscious to have greater control.

Values: Primary, singular concepts of regulation of behaviour that go to make up beliefs.

Veganism: The practice of living a cruelty-free lifestyle. Vegans do not eat, wear or use any kind of animal-based products.

Visualisation: The process of constructing imaginary pictures in your mind. It is a virtual reality experience created by one's own psychology, as if a film was playing inside your head or even on a screen outside your head, with your eyes open.

Bibliography

ANDREAS, STEVE & ANDREAS, CONNIRAE, **CHANGE YOUR MIND AND KEEP THE CHANGE**, REAL PEOPLE PRESS, USA, 1987.

BANDURA, ALBERT & WALTERS, RICHARD H, **SOCIAL LEARNING AND PERSONALITY DEVELOPMENT**, HOLT, RINEHART AND WINSTON, NEW YORK & LONDON, 1963.

BLYTHE, PETER, **SELF-HYPNOTISM**, ARTHUR BARKER, LONDON, 1976.

BRENNAN, BARBARA ANN, **HANDS OF LIGHT: A GUIDE TO HEALING THROUGH THE HUMAN ENERGY FIELD**, BANTAM BOOKS, NEW YORK, 1987.

CARROLL, LEWIS, **ALICE'S ADVENTURES IN WONDERLAND & THROUGH THE LOOKING GLASS**, PUFFIN BOOKS, UK, 1986.

CAIRNEY, EDWARD, **THE SPROUTER'S HANDBOOK**, ARGYLL PUBLISHING, ARGYLL, SCOTLAND, 1997.

COLEMAN, VERNON, **POWER OVER CANCER: DISCOVER HOW YOU CAN CUT YOUR RISK OF CANCER BY UP TO 80%**, EUROPEAN MEDICAL JOURNAL, PUBLISHING HOUSE, DEVON, UK, 1996.

CROCE, PIETRO, **VIVISECTION OR SCIENCE: AN INVESTIGATION INTO TESTING DRUGS AND SAFEGUARDING HEALTH**, ZED BOOKS, LONDON & NEW YORK, 1999.

CROOKS, ROBERT L, & STEIN, JEAN, **PSYCHOLOGY, SCIENCE, BEHAVIOUR AND LIFE**, HOLT, RINEHART AND WINSTON, USA, 1988.

DO OR DIE COLLECTIVE, **DO OR DIE: VOICES FROM THE ECOLOGICAL RESISTANCE**, NO 8, DO OR DIE, BRIGHTON, UK, 1999.

ERICKSON, MILTON H, & ROSSI, ERNEST L, **EXPERIENCING HYPNOSIS: THERAPEUTIC APPROACHES TO ALTERED STATES**, IRVINGTON PUBLISHERS, NEW YORK, 1981.

FRANKEN, ROBERT E, **HUMAN MOTIVATION: THIRD EDITION**, BROOKS/COLE PUBLISHING COMPANY, CA, USA, 1994.

Bibliography

GAULD, ALAN, **A HISTORY OF HYPNOTISM**, CAMBRIDGE UNIVERSITY PRESS, UK, 1993.

HAMMOND, D CORYDON, **HANDBOOK OF HYPNOTIC SUGGESTIONS AND METAPHORS**, AIH, CA, USA, 1990.

KAPPAS, JOHN G, PhD, **PROFESSIONAL HYPNOTISM MANUAL**, PANORAMA PUBLISHING CO, CA, USA, 1987.

KING, MARK E & CITRENBAUM, CHARLES M, **EXISTENTIAL HYPNOTHERAPY**, THE GUILDFORD PRESS, NEW YORK, 1993.

KORN, ERROL R & JOHNSON, KAREN, **VISUALIZATION: THE USES OF IMAGERY IN THE HEALTH PROFESSIONS**, DOW JONES-IRWIN, ILLINOIS, USA, 1983.

LEARY, TIMOTHY, **CHAOS & CYBERCULTURE**, RONIN PUBLISHING, CA, USA, 1994.

LYNN, STEVEN JAY & RHUE, JUDITH W, **DISSOCIATION: CLINICAL & THEORETICAL PERSPECTIVES**, THE GUILDFORD PRESS, NEW YORK, 1994.

MACHOVEC, FRANK J, PhD, ABPH, **HYPNOSIS COMPLICATIONS: PREVENTION AND RISK MANAGEMENT**, CHARLES C THOMAS PUBLISHER, ILLINOIS, USA, 1986.

MORAN, VICTORIA, **COMPASSION: THE ULTIMATE ETHIC**, AMERICAN VEGAN SOCIETY, USA, 1997.

MURRAY, MICHAEL T, ND, **HEART DISEASE AND HIGH BLOOD PRESSURE**, PRIMA PUBLISHING, USA, 1997.

O'KEEFE, TRACIE, **INVESTIGATING STAGE HYPNOSIS**, EXTRAORDINARY PEOPLE PRESS, LONDON, UK, 1998.

ROSE, COLIN, **ACCELERATED LEARNING**, ACCELERATED LEARNING SYSTEMS, BUCKS, UK, 1985.

SAFFREY, JILL & STEWART, MICHAEL (EDS), **MAINTAINING THE WHOLE: HUMAN HEALTH & BIOLOGY BOOK 3**, THE OPEN UNIVERSITY, LONDON, 1997.

SALLEH, ARIEL, **ECOFEMINISM AS POLITICS**, ZED BOOKS, LONDON &

NEW YORK, 1997.

SINGER, JEROME L & POPE, KENNETH S, **THE POWER OF HUMAN IMAG-INATION: NEW METHODS IN PSYCHOTHERAPY**, PLENUM PUBLISHING, NEW YORK, 1978.

SINGER, PETER, **ANIMAL LIBERATION**, RANDOM HOUSE, LONDON, 1975.

SMITH, TONY, MD (MEDICAL EDITOR), **THE BRITISH MEDICAL ASSOCIA-TION COMPLETE FAMILY HEALTH ENCYCLOPAEDIA**, DORLING KINDER-SLEY, LONDON, 1994.

TEBBETTS, CHARLES, **SELF-HYPNOSIS AND OTHER MIND EXPANDING TECHNIQUES**, WESTWOOD PUBLISHING COMPANY, USA, 1987.

TORTORA, GERALD J & GRABOWSKI, SANDRA REYNOLDS, **PRINCIPLES OF ANATOMY AND PHYSIOLOGY: EIGHTH EDITION**, HARPER COLLINS COLLEGE PUBLISHERS, USA, 1996.

WISE, STEVEN M, **RATTLING THE CAGE: TOWARDS LEGAL RIGHTS FOR ANIMALS**, PERSEUS BOOKS, USA, 2000.

JOURNALS AND NEWSPAPERS

BARNARD, NEAL & ESSELSTYN, CARL JR, **VEGETARIAN DIETS FLEX THEIR MUSCLES IN NEW RESEARCH**, GOOD MEDICINE, PHYSICIANS COMMITTEE FOR RESPONSIBLE MEDICINE, WASHINGTON, USA, VOL 8, NO 4, AUTUMN 1999.

BLUNKELL, CHRIS, **HYPNOTHERAPY: MUMBO JUMBO OR MIRACLE CURE?** STOP MAGAZINE, WHITSTABLE, KENT, UK, ISSUE 2, MARCH 1999.

DING, MASTER JOHN (ED), **TAI CHI & ALTERNATIVE HEALTH**, TAI CHI WORLDWIDE, LONDON, ISSUE 15, 1998.

DR HADWEN TRUST FOR HUMANE RESEARCH, **MILLENNIUM REVIEW**, HERTS, UK, 2000.

HART, DYANA, **FOOD ADDITIVES HEALTH ALERT**, KINDRED SPIRIT, TOTNES, UK, ISSUE 46, SPRING 1999.

LEAN, GEOFFREY & KOENIG, PETER, **GM BOSSES WANT TO PULL OUT OF**

Bibliography

UK, THE INDEPENDENT ON SUNDAY, UK, 5 SEPTEMBER 1999.

SCHNEIDER, MEIR & GALLUP, CAROL, **PUSHING BACK THE BOUNDARIES OF AGEING**, KINDRED SPIRIT, TOTNES, UK, ISSUE 43, SUMMER 1998.

WALKER, STELLA, **BREATH & THE MIND**, YOGA & HEALTH, YOGA TODAY, LEWES, UK, JUNE 1999.

Exercises

The following are a variety of exercises, both classical and specially designed for this book, to help you to explore your own self-concepts and actions. As discussed in the main text we all, at times, walk around acting out our lives, often without giving sufficient thought to how our actions affect ourselves, others, society, creatures and the environment – yes we are in a trance.

We do not mean to be ignorant or blind to the consequences of some of our actions but have got into a number of automatic habits that turn us into robots going about our business without really thinking things through.

In order to examine our values, beliefs, attitudes, thoughts, emotions, drives, motives and actions, it is sometimes useful and therapeutic to write them down. This can give us great clarity and understanding, further affording us the advantage of being able to logically work out ways we can go forward positively and constructively.

It is not always necessary for a person to understand their motivation in order to change, but it does help at times. This is a very important part of the book because it is teaching you to think consciously about what you can feed back into your unconscious. Take your time completing the exercises and use the information you gather to help plan suggestions you make to yourself, and the trances you create and recreate in self-hypnosis.

Who am I?

Write out 20 short statements beginning with "I am", describing who and what you are, remembering to be honest. From time to time we all need to review our life situation and such an exercise is very noble and humbling, so take pride in its completion.

1.

2.

3.

4.

5.

6.

7.

8.

9.

10.

11.

12.

13.

14.

15.

16.

17.

18.

19.

20.

Achievements

Describe the 10 most important achievements in your life so far.

1.

2.

3.

4.

5.

6.

7.

8.

9.

10.

Values

Write out 10 values on the left-hand side of the page that you think are or could help the guiding principles by which to live your life. Be sure to be honest with yourself in that they need to pertain to your life. If you think there are other values that you have not had so far in your life, that you now wish to adopt, it is OK to replace old values with these new ones. List these 10 values intuitively.

Take a short break, a breath of fresh air, and then rearrange the values on the left-hand side in order of priority on the right-hand side. Put the most important values at the top of the list and then in descending order of importance.

When you have completed the exercise, go back to the section in the book on installation of values in trance. Either do the installation by using a tape recording or write out a trance script, memorise it and use self-hypnosis.

1.	1.
2.	2.
3.	3.
4.	4.
5.	5.
6.	6.
7.	7.
8.	8.
9.	9.
10.	10.

Looking at present beliefs and installing new ones

Take time to think about the kind of beliefs about yourself that you are carrying around with you in your backpack of life. Write six of the strongest ones in the spaces below. Be sure that these are the kind of beliefs that you think are driving the way you think, behave, speak and are the under-pinning forces in the way you lead your life.

When you have written them all down, remembering to be honest, imagine you were advising a friend and ask yourself: *Would those beliefs really get that person where they want to go?*

1.

2.

3.

4.

5.

6.

Now change those beliefs to more positive constructive concepts about yourself. Remember, if you were advising a friend: *Would these concepts get them to where they want to go?*

When you have all six positive constructive beliefs that will get you where you want to go, review the main text on how you install beliefs in trance, then write a script that will install them into your unconscious mind.

1.

2.

3.

4.

5.

6.

Scanning for *Me* diseases

L ife always has at least two different perspectives: hot-cold, dry-wet, calm-angry, positive-negative. Negative *Me* diseases are old thought and action strategies that once served a purpose, but became out of date and stuck, like an old scratched record going round and round on the turntable.

Go into a trance, review your life and identify 10 *Me* diseases that you think you may have suffered from, write them out and check with two independent friends to see if they agree. When you have completed all 10, linguistically convert the *Me* diseases into positive constructive statements, using the formula discussed in the main text, making a second list.

1.	6.
2.	7.
3.	8.
4.	9.
5.	10.

Positive statements

1.

2.

3.

4.

5.

6.

7.

8.

9.

10.

Attitudes

Ask three sincere friends to sum up below their opinion of your attitudes towards yourself, life, other people, and how you could improve those attitudes. Ask them to be constructive in their criticism of your behaviour.

This is a more difficult exercise because in some ways you lay yourself open to other people's views of you that they would perhaps not normally share in polite society. It will teach you how to respond constructively towards constructive criticism.

1.

2.

3.

Devise suggestions which can be used in a script that will help you change your attitudes to be more constructive, taking on board any constructive criticism above, checking that your new attitudes are congruent with your values and beliefs about yourself.

Awakening your untapped potential

As you are aware by now, going through this book, I have a belief that you are only scratching the surface of your innate human potential. I know you are more intelligent than you used to think you are. Take this time to write out a description of 10 abilities that you have not yet developed in your life and which you may look at expanding as you grow.

1.

2.

3.

4.

5.

6.

7.

8.

9.

10.

What I want in and from my life: Goal discovery, setting and installation

Write out 75 things that you want in or from life. Continue until you have filled the whole of the spaces. Some things can be important, some can be not so important, but nevertheless make sure you fill the whole 75 spaces. When you have completed the first part of the task, take a break, then come back and distil the list down to 20 and finally down to five of the most important things.

Take your time with this exercise; there is no rush or hurry, even doing it over different sessions if you would like. When you have your final list, write out a trance script to ask your unconscious to help you find ways to plan strategies to assist you in reaching your goals, bearing in mind your life's values, guiding principles, beliefs and attitudes.

1.	26.	51.
2.	27.	52.
3.	28.	53.
4.	29.	54.
5.	30.	55.
6.	31.	56.
7.	32.	57.
8.	33.	58.
9.	34.	59.
10.	35.	60.
11.	36.	61.
12.	37.	62.
13.	38.	63.
14.	39.	64.
15.	40.	65.
16.	41.	66.
17.	42.	67.
18.	43.	68.
19.	44.	69.
20.	45.	70.
21.	46.	71.
22.	47.	72.
23.	48.	73.
24.	49.	74.
25.	50.	75.

Reduce your list to the 20 most important things.

1.
2.
3.
4.
5.
6.
7.
8.
9.
10.
11.
12.
13.
14.
15.
16.
17.
18.
19.
20.

Reduce your list to the five most important things

1.
2.
3.
4.
5.

Memorise the list, go into a trance and ask your unconscious to guide you towards getting those five most important things in your life in a way that is right for you, taking into account your values, guiding principles, beliefs, and attitudes.

Visualising a perfect place in your mind

Create inside your mind, when you are in trance, three images of perfection with visualisation, sound, feelings, smell and taste. Crystallise those experiences and write them out as you have experienced them.

1. Place of ultimate peace

2. Place of laughter and happiness

3. Place of confidence

Write out a script to use in trance to blend all three together to create the place of absolute safety and pleasure in your mind to go to whenever you need, want or desire.

How, what, where, when and why

The five w's can be important questions to ask yourself when embarking on a task. People often go into a situation unprepared, not having rehearsed what they will do to handle any situation that arises. Photocopy the page and before you go into any important situation, write out the five w's then ask yourself in trance: *Is this is really the right thing for me to do?*

How

What

Where

When

Why

Looking at food

In a busy world where many demands are made on an individual, eating often becomes automatic without a person really considering what is passing their lips and going into their bodies. By filling in the details below you can seriously consider how to eat your way to 100 years old with raw food veganism.

List below 50 convenience or cooked foods you used to eat, noting the following details of each item:

Name of food
Whether it has carbohydrate, lipid (fats or oils) or protein content
Its vitamin and mineral content
Its medicinal properties
Any health drawbacks

1.
2.
3.
4.
5.
6.
7.
8.
9.
10.
11.
12.
13.
14.
15.
16.
17.
18.
19.
20.
21.
22.
23.
24.
25.
26.
27.

28.
29.
30.
31.
32.
33.
34.
35.
36.
37.
38.
39.
40.
41.
42.
43.
44.
45.
46.
47.
48.
49.
50.

In writing out the second half of this exercise I want you to think before you eat, using your mind before your mouth. Remember, calorie content is not an issue with raw vegan food because your digestive system immediately processes its contents and there is no constipation. This means there is less need for storage of energy as body fat.

List below 50 of the unprocessed, raw foods you can eat, noting the following details of each one:

Name of food
Whether it has carbohydrate, lipid (fats or oils) or protein content
Its vitamin and mineral content
Its medicinal properties
Any health drawbacks

1.
2.
3.
4.
5.

6.
7.
8.
9.
10.
11.
12.
13.
14.
15.
16.
17.
18.
19.
20.
21.
22.
23.
24.
25.
26.
27.
28.
29.
30.
31.
32.
33.
34.
35.
36.
37.
38.
39.
40.
41.
42.
43.
44.
45.
46.
47.
48.

49.

50.

Write out suggestions that will reflect your new realisation and attitude towards food. Create a self-hypnosis script reflecting what you have learned and how that can be used in the way you think before you eat, and shop more than you cook.

Working for the other creatures on the planet

Go into a trance and imagine that you are working as an animal rights campaigner. Your aim is to stop the torture of animals in laboratories, improve their living conditions by returning them to the wild whenever possible, prevent them from being murdered for food and clothing, and prevent their skins being used as adornments, and their use in entertainment.

Write out four arguments why you would be right to ask for those things on behalf of the animals that cannot speak for themselves.

State your scientific argument

What is your moral reasoning?

What would be your nutritional argument?

How do you respond in a positive constructive way to people who think you are a crackpot?

Go into trance and imagine that you were that campaigner for a day.

What I am doing to make the planet a better place to live

Over the past few hundred years the planet and wildlife have been devastated by the actions of the industrialised world. You can remember life is not all about what you need or want.

Write out 10 actions you are currently and will be carrying out to redress the balance of nature and restore the Gaia theory (the idea that the planet is a living organism, of which we are all a part, which creates the balance of the living, integrated eco-system).

When you have written them out, turn each one into a suggestion, writing them into a trance to ensure you carry out those actions.

1.

2.

3.

4.

5.

6.

7.

8.

9.

10.

Asking for a better world

Just imagine that you were going to vote for the Green Party at your local elections. What 10 radical policies would you want them to implement if they got into power? Make the answers different from your 10 personal actions to improve the world.

When you have finished the statements, photocopy them and send them off to each of the political parties in your area.

Remember: every revolution starts from the bottom upwards – your vote and opinions count.

1.

2.

3.

4.

5.

6.

7.

8.

9.

10.

Acts of Kindness

Write out 20 acts of kindness that you can complete during the next month, without expecting anything in return, and schedule them. The recipients of those acts do not necessarily have to know that you are carrying them out.

1.

2.

3.

4.

5.

6.

7.

8.

9.

10.

11.

12.

13.

14.

15.

16.

17.

18.

19.

20.

What is confidence to you...*NOW!*

If you have completed most of the exercises in this book, you will have changed a great deal as a person – that is inevitable because the book and self-hypnosis provoke unconscious and conscious change.

Describe what confidence begins with and why.

How do you stand and hold yourself when you are confident?

What is specific about a confident person's breathing?

How does a confident person's face look?

What images is the confident person experiencing about themselves inside their own mind?

Why does confidence always have to include kindness?

Why do confident people constantly reprogramme their psychological well being?

When and where can you be confident and under what circumstances?

Write a self-hypnosis script based on your comments.

Seminars and Lectures

By Dr Tracie O'Keefe DCH

Tracie is a qualified and registered clinical hypnotherapist, psychotherapist, counsellor and trainer at the London Medical Centre, Harley Street. She trained with the National School of Hypnosis and Advanced Psychotherapy in London. Her degree, as well as her doctorate in clinical hypnotherapy, was earned at the American Institute of Hypnotherapy in the USA and issued in co-ordination with the state of California.

Further to this she has trained at other colleges and schools, including the Open University, and constantly spends a lot of her time on developing her skills as a therapist. For over 20 years she has been helping people empower themselves and achieve their goals.

With a wealth of experience in the field of personal and sexual identity, she both writes and speaks on the subject. She is the internationally successful author of the books, **Trans-X-U-All: The Naked Difference** and **Sex, Gender & Sexuality: 21st Century Transformations**, and has taught in the field of sex, sexuality and gender in the National Health Service (UK).

Her special project has been the development of the **Pan-identity Model of Sex, Gender and Sexuality**, and her work has been reviewed in several international academic publications, including *the European Journal of Clinical Hypnosis* and *The Psychotherapist*. Far from being a stuffy lecturer, she is a vibrant and engaging speaker who is fascinated and devoted to human development through therapeutic approaches combined with hypnosis. Tracie is also the author of **Investigating Stage Hypnosis**.

Tracie is available for talks, seminars and workshops. For further details or enquiries, please contact her via Turnaround Publisher Services on:

Tel. 020 8829 3000 Fax. 020 8881 5088
E-mail bill@turnaround-uk.com
Website: http://easyweb.easynet.co.uk/~katfox/tracie1.htm

Trans-X-U-All
The Naked Difference
By Tracie O'Keefe and Katrina Fox
Foreword by April Ashley

Please send me..........copies of the above book, which is a comprehensive overview of the transsexual experience. I attach payment totalling.............Cheques made payable to **Turnaround Publisher Services**, which includes postage and packing.

NAME.. . . . . Address
. . . . .
Town. . . . . Zip/Post code. . . . .
Country. . . . .

If you are paying by credit card please fill in the following details:
Name of card holder. . . . . Card
no . . . . Statement
address. . . . .
Town . . . . .Zip/Post code. . . . .
Country. . . . . .Date of card issue. . . . . . .
Date of expiry. . . . . SIGNATURE. . . . .

VISA/DELTA/MASTERCARD/EUROCARD CARDS ACCEPTED

Please allow 28 days for delivery. Mail to Turnaround Publisher Services, Unit 3, Olympia Trading Estate, Coburg Rd, London N22 6TZ. Price £11.99. Postage £2.00 plus £0.50 per book. For overseas prices contact the Customer Service Department on tel: 020 8829 3000, or fax 020 8881 5088 or e-mail orders@turnaround-uk.com

More information at:
http://easyweb.easynet.co.uk/~katfox/tran1.htm

Reviews

An absolutely fascinating book
April Ashley

A very detailed and well researched book
The Tranny Guide 1997

The most thorough and practical guide to gender dysphoria
Gems News

The most important book on earth
TV/TS London News

Fascinating and eminently readable
TransEssex International

Every time I put it down, somebody pinches it
Luisa Dillner, Health Editor, The Guardian and British Medical Journal

An excellent book
Press for Change

An enlightening layperson's guide to the transsexual experience
Gay Times

Useful reading, particularly for teachers of human development and therapists dealing with clients questioning their identity
The Psychotherapist (Journal of the United Kingdom Council for Psychotherapists)

A fascinating, useful resource on an interesting subject, accessible to all
Nursing Times

Very readable, sound information given with some humour
European Journal of Clinical Hypnosis

Investigating Stage Hypnosis

By Tracie O'Keefe

Foreword by Margaret Harper (Campaign Against Stage Hypnosis)

Please send me..........copies of the above book, which is a comprehensive overview of stage hypnosis. I attach payment totalling.............Cheques made payable to **Turnaround Publisher Services**, which includes postage and packing.

NAME.. . . . . Address
. . . .
Town. . . . . Zip/Post code. . . . .
Country. . . . .

If you are paying by credit card please fill in the following details:
Name of card holder. . . . . Card
no . . . . Statement
address. . . . .
Town . . . . .Zip/Post code. . . . .
Country . . . . .Date of card issue. . . . . . .
Date of expiry. . . . . SIGNATURE. . . . .

VISA/DELTA/MASTERCARD/EUROCARD CARDS ARE ACCEPTED

Please allow 28 days for delivery. Mail to Turnaround Publisher Services, Unit 3, Olympia Trading Estate, Coburg Rd, London N22 6TZ. Price £11.99. Postage £2.00 plus £0.50 per book. For overseas prices contact the Customer Service Department on tel: 020 8829 3000, or fax 020 8881 5088 or e-mail orders@turnaround-uk.com

More information at:
http://easyweb.easynet.co.uk/~katfox/stage1.htm

Reviews

This is a very important book. I congratulate the author for her courage and hard work
Dr Basil Finer, MD, PhD, Journal of European Society of Hypnosis in Psychotherapy and Psychosomatic Medicine

A powerful and revealing exposé
Margaret Harper, Campaign Against Stage Hypnosis

A controversial book, which deserves to be read by every hypnotherapist
Dr Morris Berg PhD, National Association of Counsellors, Hypnotherapists, and Psychotherapists

Well put together and easy to read
Derek Crussell, South London Hypnotherapy Practice

It's about time someone wrote a book like this
Dr Prem Misra, psychiatrist and past president of the British Society of Medical and Dental Hypnosis, Scotland

A very comprehensive book
Steve Jones, LBC Radio

An astounding piece of work
Dr Caroline Miller, American Institute of Hypnotherapy, on the thesis that formed the basis of this book

Sex, Gender & Sexuality

21st Century Transformations
By Dr Tracie O'Keefe DCH

Please send me..........copies of the above book, which is a comprehensive overview of the world of the sex, gender and sexuality diverse. I attach payment totalling.............Cheques made payable to **Turnaround Publisher Services**, which includes postage and packing.

NAME.. . . . . **Address**
. . . .
Town. . . . . **Zip/Post code**. . . . .
Country. . . . .

If you are paying by credit card please fill in the following details:
Name of card holder. . . . .**Card**
no . . . . **Statement**
address. . . . .
Town . . . .**Zip/Post code**. . . . .
Country. . . . .**Date of card issue**. . . . . . .
Date of expiry. . . . . **SIGNATURE**. . . . .

Only VISA/DELTA/MASTERCARD CARDS ARE ACCEPTED

VISA/DELTA/MASTERCARD/EUROCARD CARDS ARE ACCEPTED

Please allow 28 days for delivery. Mail to Turnaround Publisher Services, Unit 3, Olympia Trading Estate, Coburg Rd, London N22 6TZ. Price £11.99. Postage £2.00 plus £0.50 per book. For overseas prices contact the Customer Service Department on tel: 020 8829 3000, or fax 020 8881 5088 or e-mail orders@turnaround-uk.com

More information at:
http://easyweb.easynet.co.uk/~katfox/21st.htm

Reviews

This is a well researched book that advocates liberty for sexual minorities
Alice Purnell, BSc, RGN, PGCC, Gendys Network

An incisive insight into the complete scale of sex, gender and sexuality
Yvonne Williams, Editor, Reflections International (Trans-Essex)

A valiant and courageous attempt to help us become more in-tune and empowered within ourselves – the reading of this book is a must for everyone of us
Dr Napewastewin Schutzer PhD, Gems News, journal of the Gender Trust

A very good book and so easy to understand
Petra Klene, Humanitas, Netherlands

A worthy successor to Trans-X-U-All
Alex Whinnom, Press for Change

All I can say is WOW!
Vanessa Murray, International Foundation for Gender Education, USA

Nuggets of prize information and encyclopaedic knowledge from Dr O'Keefe, who obviously lives and breathes her work
Time Out

Self-Hypnosis for Life
Mind, Body & Spiritual Excellence
By Dr Tracie O'Keefe DCH

Please send me..........copies of the above book, which is a comprehensive overview of self-hypnosis. I attach payment totalling.............Cheques made payable to **Turnaround Publisher Services**, which includes postage and packing.

NAME.. . . . . **Address**
. . . .
Town. . . . . **Zip/Post code**. . . . .
Country. . . . .

If you are paying by credit card please fill in the following details:
Name of card holder. . . . . **Card**
no . . . . **Statement**
address. . . . .
Town . . . .**Zip/Post code**. . . . .
Country . . . .**Date of card issue**. . . . . . .
Date of expiry. . . . . **SIGNATURE**. . . . .

VISA/DELTA/MASTERCARD/EUROCARD CARDS ARE ACCEPTED

Please allow 28 days for delivery. Mail to Turnaround Publisher Services, Unit 3, Olympia Trading Estate, Coburg Rd, London N22 6TZ. Price £11.99. Postage £2.00 plus £0.50 per book. For overseas prices contact the Customer Service Department on tel: 020 8829 3000, or fax 020 8881 5088 or e-mail orders@turnaround-uk.com

More information at:
http://easyweb.easynet.co.uk/~katfox/self.htm

Index